MAP OF
ANCIENT
ROME

MAIN SIGHTS

1. **Aqueduct of Nero**: *for aqueducts, see pages 6-7 and 14-15*

2. **Baths of Titus**: *pages 14-15*

3. **Trajan's Baths**: *pages 14-15*

4. **Subura District**: *pages 16-17*

5. **Roman Forum**: *pages 20-21*

6. **Imperial Fora**: *pages 22-23*

7. **Colosseum**: *pages 24-25*

8. **Circus Maximus**: *pages 26-27*

9. **Theatrum Marcelli**: *pages 28-29*

10. **Theatrum Pompei**: *pages 28-29*

11. **Pantheon**: *pages 30-31*

12. **Via Sacra**: *pages 32-33*

13. **Arch of Titus**: *pages 32-33*

14. **Arch of Augustus**: *pages 32-33*

15. **Via Appia**: *see pages 34-35*

16. **Port of Rome**: *pages 42-43*

17. **Forum Boarium**: *pages 42-43*

18. **Forum Holitorium**: *pages 42-43*

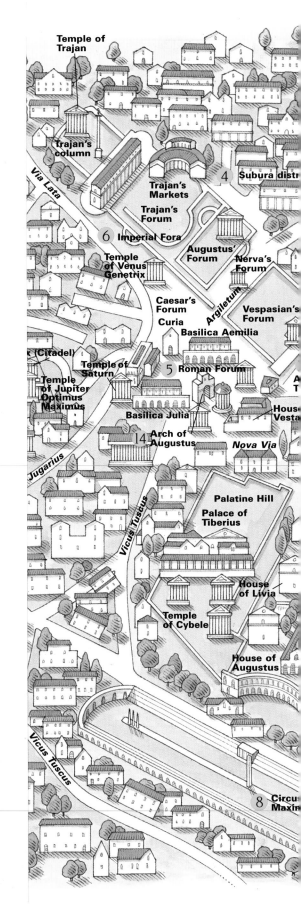

Temple of Trajan

Via Lata

Trajan's column

Trajan's Markets

Trajan's Forum

4 Subura distr

6 Imperial Fora

Augustus' Forum

Nerva's Forum

Temple of Venus Genetrix

Caesar's Forum

Curia

Argiletum

Vespasian's Forum

Basilica Aemilia

k (Citadel)

Temple of Jupiter Optimus Maximus

Temple of Saturn

5 Roman Forum

Basilica Julia

14 Arch of Augustus

Nova Via

House Vesta

Jugarius

Vicus Tuscus

Palatine Hill

Palace of Tiberius

House of Livia

Temple of Cybele

House of Augustus

Vicus Tuscus

8 Circus Maxin

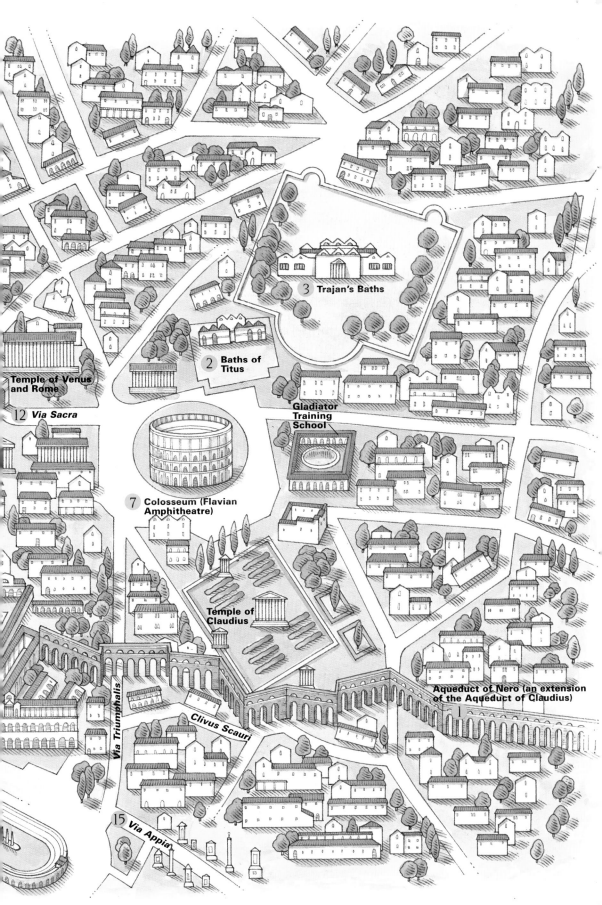

3 Trajan's Baths

2 Baths of Titus

Temple of Venus and Rome

12 *Via Sacra*

Gladiator Training School

7 Colosseum (Flavian Amphitheatre)

Temple of Claudius

Via Triumphalis

Clivus Scauri

Aqueduct of Nero (an extension of the Aqueduct of Claudius)

15 *Via Appia*

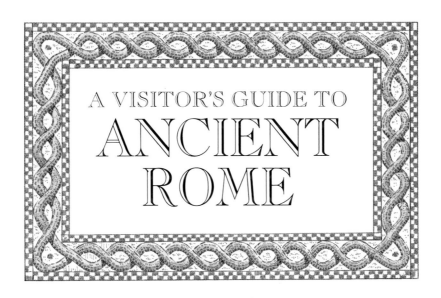

A VISITOR'S GUIDE TO
ANCIENT ROME

Lesley Sims

Illustrated by Christyan Fox,
Ian Jackson & John Woodcock

Designed by Lucy Parris
Edited by Jane Chisholm

History consultant: Dr Anne Millard

CONTENTS

Introduction:

3   The city of Rome
4   About this guide

Tourist information:

6   Where to stay
8   Eating and drinking
10   The evening meal
12   Bathing
14   Water palaces
16   Out and about
18   Getting sick

Sightseeing:

20   The Roman Forum
22   The Imperial Fora
24   The Colosseum
26   Chariot racing
28   Seeing a play
30   Architectural art
32   Military processions
34   Tombs and catacombs

Shopping:

36   Day-to-day shopping
38   A shopper's paradise
40   Markets
42   The Port of Rome

Trips out of Rome:

44   Ostia
46   A week in the country

Background:

48   Religion and festivals
50   Fashion
52   Education
54   The army
56   Useful information
58   Phrasebook
59   Useful definitions
60   Who's who
        in Ancient Rome
62   Timeline
64   Index

With thanks to: Nicola Hanna and the Bedford Museum;
Ron Sims; Jenny Hall, Museum of London.

First published in 1999 by Usborne Publishing Limited,
83-85 Saffron Hill, London EC1N 8RT, England.
Copyright © 1999 Usborne Publishing Limited. The
name Usborne and the device ⊕ are Trade Marks of
Usborne Publishing Limited.
UE First published in America in 2000.

THE CITY OF ROME

Rome sits in the middle of Italy, which is itself at the heart of the Mediterranean, in southern Europe. Right in the middle of an Etruscan* trade route, Rome was destined to become a great Empire from the beginning. It started as a group of villages on hills, by the banks of the Tiber where the river was easiest to cross.

ITALY

Rome is located just 25kms (about 15 miles) from the coast.

Rome

Ostia

Naples

Capri

ORIGINS

Early settlements were wooden huts, built on seven hills for protection against the weather and the enemy. Some of these have been dated back to the 10th century BC. According to legend though, the city was founded in 753BC. This may well be when the villages merged into a town – but the rest of the story is pure fiction.

The 'Seven Hills' of Rome, surrounded by the Servian Wall, which enclosed the early city.

The Servian Wall

Quirinal Hill

Viminal Hill

Capitoline Hill

Esquiline Hill

Tiber

Forum

Palatine Hill

Caelian Hill

Aventine Hill

Via Appia

ONCE UPON A TIME...

... twin boys called Romulus and Remus were cast into the Tiber by a wicked uncle, who had murdered their grandfather and stolen his throne. The boys drifted to a marshy area under the Capitoline Hill, where they were washed ashore and suckled by a she-wolf.

Years later, Mars (the god of War) told them to build a city where they'd been abandoned. But during the founding ceremony, Remus ridiculed the boundary wall. In a rage, Romulus killed him, and became the sole ruler of the city he named Rome.

This bronze statue of a she-wolf may be Etruscan. Romulus and Remus are later additions.

* The Etruscans lived in north-west Italy and had a thriving civilization before the Romans.

ABOUT THIS GUIDE

This is a guide to what you'd find if you were to travel back to the Roman Empire in 118AD. The Empire lasted for another 400 years, but this was when it was at its height, at the end of the emperor Trajan's reign and the start of Hadrian's. Emperors, beginning with Augustus, had been ruling for just over one hundred years and the population of Rome had exploded to more than one million people (which was huge for an ancient city).

You can find information on where to stay and what to eat, sightseeing suggestions, ideas for trips out of Rome and a useful map of the city. At the back are historical background details on topics such as fashion and religion, plus notes on currency and a handy phrasebook.

VISA INFORMATION

The good news is, you won't need a visa – or even a passport. Rome welcomes everyone. Since the Empire's expansion, people from dozens of countries make up its population. All that's required is loyalty to the emperor and respect for the Roman way of life.

The Empire reached its largest extent with Trajan's defeat of Dacia (present-day Romania).

TOURIST TIPS

On most pages, there are helpful hints for things to do and how to behave. They're shown in boxes like the one below, which has probably the most important tip of all.

> **TOP TIPS FOR TOURISTS**
> **No. 1: Citizenship**
>
> Whatever else you forget, REMEMBER THIS VITAL PHRASE: *"Civis Romanus sum"* (say *Key-wiss Row*, as in boat, *mar-nuss sum*). It means, "I am a Roman citizen". Roman citizens have more rights than anyone else. So even if the phrase can't get you out of trouble, it will certainly ensure that the trouble is less severe.

The Roman Empire in 117AD: the Romans control most of Europe and beyond.

Occupied territories

Fortified walls to keep out enemies

BRITAIN GERMANY

Atlantic Ocean

GAUL

ITALY

Black Sea

DACIA

Rome

ASIA

Corsica

SPAIN

Sardinia

Mediterranean Sea

Sicily

GREECE

Aegean Sea

Crete

Cyprus

EGYPT

AFRICA

QUIRKY QUOTES

Some pages also have quotes from 'visitors' to Rome or locals, including well-known contemporary authors. Quotes are shown like this:

66 *The quotes give useful insights but they are personal opinions which don't necessarily reflect the viewpoints of the writers of this guide.* **99**

WHAT TO WEAR

Rome is generally warm with mild showers, but insufferably hot during June, July and August. You'll be able to buy tunics and sandals from the markets and it's a good idea to head there first. Though you may prefer shorts and a T-shirt, you'll attract attention. If you really want to blend in, buy a robe called a toga, only worn by citizens. (See page 50 for tips on wearing it.)

DRINKING WATER

In such heat, you'll probably drink a lot and the usual canned drinks aren't an option. There are no useful refrigerated drinks stands on hand either. So take a water bottle with you – you can fill it at one of the hundreds of public fountains dotted around the city. The water is perfectly safe to drink. It's piped in from rivers and springs outside the city (see pages 7 and 9).

ARRIVING

Like many others, Rome is a city of great contrasts, from wealth to grinding poverty, and in common with every other city, it never stops. Everyone's first impressions are different but, as you arrive, several things will hit you in the face. There's the heat, the noise, crowded streets with no cars, and the overpowering smell of food being cooked. On top of that, everyone will be speaking in Latin. After taking a few minutes to accustom yourself to your new surroundings, take the plunge. The first thing you'll need to organize is somewhere to stay.

THE FAST-MOVING CITY

Rome is constantly changing, with new buildings going up all the time, so some of the things you read about may be different by the time you arrive. If you have any updates, or other comments or information to share, please write to the address at the front of this guide.

Old buildings are torn down and new ones erected, as each emperor puts his mark on the city.

WHERE TO STAY

A lthough Rome has tens of thousands of visitors a year, their expectations are probably much lower than yours. Modern day tourists are likely to find Rome's inns less than satisfactory. Some aren't respectable, or even clean. Facilities will be basic and the atmosphere rowdy, to say the least.

RENTING

Your best bet is to try to rent somewhere – an apartment in an *insula* (block) if money's tight; a *domus* (town house) if you're feeling rich. Many wealthy Romans move out to country villas during the summer, which should help your search. But bear in mind that, if you want a *domus*, there are only 2,000 in all of Rome, whereas there are more than 47,000 *insulae**.

The higher you go, the more crowded the apartment block. With rent so high, Romans rent out rooms to other families.

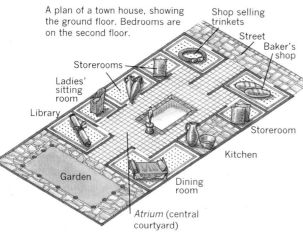

A plan of a town house, showing the ground floor. Bedrooms are on the second floor.

Shop selling trinkets

Street

Baker's shop

Storerooms

Ladies' sitting room

Library

Storeroom

Kitchen

Garden

Dining room

Atrium (central courtyard)

Best of all, you might be able to find an apartment belonging to a government official working in one of Rome's provinces. In that case, the flat will not only be furnished, but a cook and household staff will probably be included in the rent.

Expect to fork out a fair amount wherever you stay: buying a country estate costs the same as a year's rent on an apartment in Rome. If you do settle for an apartment, go for smaller buildings: nothing over four floors. They have fewer (noisy) tenants, are better built, and less of a fire risk.

Avoid places with shops on the ground floor and go for a ground floor apartment – these often have a kitchen and water supply. Pick one away from the markets, or the noise of carts being unloaded will keep you awake all night. (Most wheeled vehicles are only allowed to enter the city between sunset and dawn.)

* *insulae* is the plural of *insula*.

FEW AMENITIES

Luxury apartments have running water and even bathrooms, but most are mainly a place to sleep. To bathe, everyone goes to the public baths (pages 12-15); for food, they visit one of the plethora of eating places Rome has to offer (pages 8-11). Lavatories are also public, charging a nominal 1 *as* (see page 56).

SANITATION

The city's system of drainage is second to none. Seven sewers underground wash waste into the Tiber river via the massive *Cloaca Maxima* (Great Drain). This sewer, a natural waterway, was developed into a canal system by the Etruscans.

FREE-FLOWING WATER

Rome has an unrivalled water-supply in the form of 10 channels, or aqueducts, which carry a constant torrent of fresh water into the city. The penalty for blocking it is severe – a fine of up to 10,000 *sestertii*.

Communal lavatories are situated on the ground floor of some apartment buildings. They're considered sociable places to meet and chat.

TOP TIPS FOR TOURISTS
No. 2: Air freshener

Before you agree to rent anywhere, check that the landlord, or his agent, arranges for the stairs and hallways to be regularly swept and cleaned. Your rooms will still get stuffy, though. Pliny (a Roman writer and senator) burns bread in his rooms to counteract this. If you prefer the smell of charred toast to sweat, you might like to try it.

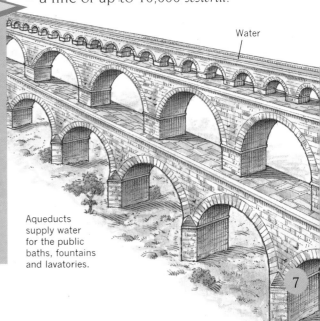

Water

Aqueducts supply water for the public baths, fountains and lavatories.

7

EATING AND DRINKING

Rome is bursting with taverns and market stalls, providing hot and cold snacks and cooked food to eat in or take home. This is one example of where an essential drawback – the fact that most apartments don't have kitchens because of the fire risk – works to the advantage of the hungry tourist.

SNACK BARS

Many people eat in the street, though most snack bars have somewhere you can sit down. Even the fussiest eater should find food he recognizes, from bread and cheese to hot pies, sausages, bacon and beans, or fried fish. As a general guide, check that the snack bar is clean and the dishes aren't swimming in olive oil.

SALADS AND SWEETS

For the health conscious, there's a wide variety of salad and vegetable dishes on offer, though vegetables are often fried or roasted. Desserts include pastries and honeycakes. There are also endless amounts of fresh fruit: melons, grapes, apples, figs, plums and pears.

THE MAIN MEAL

If the Romans bother with breakfast, it's a snack of wheat biscuits dipped in honey. Lunch can be light, perhaps bread and cheese, though some enjoy salads, eggs and cold meats. It's dinner which is the main meal of the day (see pages 10-11).

Pictures showing the food on offer are displayed on the walls outside snack bars. There are no menus – so even if your Latin is rusty, you won't order fried cow's udders by mistake.

Eating in the street, you can use your fingers, though most Romans carry their own knife and spoon with them.

Food is stored in covered jars, held in holes in the counter to keep warm.

TOP TIPS FOR TOURISTS
No. 3: Self-catering

If you get fed-up with eating out, you could buy and prepare your own food. Officially, most apartments don't have kitchens, but the previous tenants may have set up an illegal brick stove. These rest on wooden floors, so be careful not to start a fire.

Public bakeries will cook a prepared meal for you, but they charge, which is why there are so many illegal stoves and so many outbreaks of fire.

DRINKING

Wine, often spiced or sweetened with honey and generally watered down, is on sale everywhere. There are almost 200 varieties to choose from. If you'd rather have a soft drink, you can buy grape juice or honey-sweetened water. There are also dozens of public drinking fountains, continually supplied with water carried in from aqueducts outside Rome.

SEASONING

Whatever you eat, you'll find it strongly seasoned. Chefs use herbs and spices liberally, and douse most dishes in sauce. One of the most popular is the salty fish pickle sauce, *liquamen*. Be careful if you have a delicate stomach: it's very strong. (One version contains fish entrails which have been left to rot in a pot of brine for six weeks.)

Honey is used as a sweetener, not only for desserts but also with meat and fish. Concentrated wine and dried raisins are also used to enhance a dish's taste. Sugar is very expensive as it comes from India. It's never used in cooking, though it is found in some medicines.

DAILY BREAD

Bread is a staple part of the Roman diet and loaves come in a selection of sizes. You can buy them plain or with added seeds, nuts, herbs or spices. Each baker puts in his own unique blend of ingredients. Look for the distinctive pattern or mark on some loaves. Just like famous brand names, several bakers have their own mark to encourage customers to return to them.

This might look like a fancy sculpture, but it's a typical Roman drinking fountain.

THE EVENING MEAL

Dinner, or *cena*, the main meal of the day, used to be eaten as early as two-thirty in the afternoon. It's now held in the early evening, customarily after a visit to the baths. Despite the stories, not all Romans gorge themselves on lavish banquets. Many eat much plainer meals of roast poultry or fish with vegetables, followed by fresh fruit. As for the poor and slaves, they make do with wheat porridge, or *pulmentum*, a vegetable stew of peas, beans and lentils.

FEASTING FIT TO BUST

If you are invited to a banquet, leap at the chance. It's worth trying once, just for the experience. At the door, you'll be announced by a *nomenclator* (usher). Be ready to take off your sandals. Your feet must be washed by a slave before you can enter the *triclinium* (dining room). The usher will then show you to your place and a slave will come to wash your hands before the meal begins.

You may be served flamingo tongues or sow's udders with sea urchins.

Acrobats and musicians are usually on hand to amuse diners. If you're unlucky, your host will read you his poetry.

One side of the table is clear of couches for the slaves to serve from. The couch opposite seats the most important guests.

Nine is the maximum number of guests around a table.

TOP TIPS FOR TOURISTS
No. 4: Table napkins

Each diner spreads a napkin in front of him to protect the host's couch. It's a good idea to bring your own. Then you can use it to take away any leftover food.

"Seating", or rather "lying", is arranged in order of the guests' importance. All guests recline on mattresses spread with cushions. Don't ask for a chair – only slaves and young children sit to eat.

Tiny spoons are provided to eat the egg and shellfish starters.

TABLE MANNERS

Although knives and spoons are available, most people eat with their fingers. Forks are completely unheard of. Food is generally cut up before it leaves the kitchen, but eating is still a messy business. After each course, slaves will pour perfumed water over your hands and wipe them dry. Elegant toothpicks will also be offered.

Don't be surprised by the antics of fellow-diners. Not only do they spit, they show their appreciation of a meal by burping. You might try out a few rounded belches beforehand. Not burping risks insulting your host. Just remember to break the habit back home.

ON THE MENU

Arrive hungry: seven courses are the norm. You'll begin simply, with various cold dishes. After a sip of *mulsum* (honey wine), the menu gets really exotic. Most dishes are good but, even though everyone else will pile their plates high, you'd be wise to try small portions first. And don't forget to leave room for dessert. You'll probably only want one pastry though – they're sickeningly sweet.

Certain households are known for 'unusual' cuisine. Be warned: these dishes can taste truly disgusting. Roman cooks pride themselves on their ability to disguise food, so pork may look like fish or duck. In extreme cases, not recognizing what you are eating is not a bad thing.

TABLE TALK

To break the ice, compliment your host on his tablecloth if he has one. They're the latest fad, so he probably will. You'll find conversation focuses on local gossip rather than more elevated topics, and fellow guests may seem sarcastic, even blunt. Avoid arguments such as whether the Earth is round. Though the Greeks have long since discovered this, some Romans still can't believe it.

There'll also be plenty of entertainment from the hired acts – musicians and dancers, even conjurors – to provide a welcome break between courses.

MENU
Gustatio (starter)
A selection of radishes, lettuce, eggs, mushrooms, oysters, cheese and sardines
Mulsum
Entrées
Fried mullet with prawns
Mackerel in a tuna fish sauce served with hot rolls
Roasts
Roast venison with leeks fried in honey
Roast boar in liquamen sauce served with cabbage, turnips, beans and sprouts
Secundae mensae (dessert)
Honey cakes, stuffed dates, fresh fruit, including apples, pears and grapes, figs and nuts

BATHING

Rome has 11 public baths or *thermae* which are open to all and are far more than just places to bathe (see next pages). The tiled floors are probably the only thing they'll have in common with your local pool, unless that has marble pillars, high-domed ceilings and statues in every corner.

There are also several privately owned baths in Rome. These are more exclusive, offering greater privacy and sometimes special attractions such as celebrity masseurs, but they are strictly for the wealthy.

OPENING HOURS

Most public baths open around mid-morning and close at sunset. For privacy, men and women are admitted to the bathing areas at separate times of day – women in the morning, men in the afternoon.

Although in Nero's time mixed bathing was encouraged, this is strictly a thing of the past. Steer clear of baths offering mixed facilities. They're not respectable!

TOP TIPS FOR TOURISTS
No. 5: Changing rooms

If your household doesn't have a slave, hire someone at the baths to keep an eye on your things. The changing rooms don't have lockers, just unguarded shelves where everyone leaves their clothes, and thefts are common.

SOAP ON A STICK?

You can't buy soap, but there are plentiful supplies of oil, which the Romans use instead. This is smeared over your body, then scraped off (along with the grime), with a curved stick called a *strigil*.

Strigils can be rented at the baths, but they're very cheap to buy. It's probably a good idea to buy your own from one of the markets (see pages 40-1), especially if you plan to visit the baths regularly during your stay.

They're tricky to use on your own, though. Hold the bumpy end and scrape the curved part over your skin. If you can afford it, hire an attendant to scrape you off – but be warned, their services aren't cheap. The next best thing is to go with a friend and scrape each other.

A metal *strigil* – strigils can also be made of wood or bone. They're often carried on a ring like keys, with a scoop for pouring oil.

ENTRANCE FEES

Charges are a nominal *quadrans* for men. Women can pay more (up to an *as*) but for a full day's admission, including facilities, it's worth it. If money's tight, the **Baths of Agrippa** are free, and children get in free to all the baths in Rome. Wealthy citizens seeking election often pay everyone's fees for the day too.

GUIDE TO THE BATHS

The baths are made up of several rooms, customarily visited in a specific order. To get into the spirit of the thing, you can visit the on-site gym first for some weight-lifting or wrestling. If that's too energetic for you, head straight for the *apodyteria* (changing room) where you leave your clothes. The plan below gives the layout of a typical bathhouse, showing the rooms and the order you visit them.

WARNING!
Not everyone wants to see a guidebook with naked figures, so we've covered the bathers in our pictures with towels. At the baths, however, nudity is not just accepted but expected.

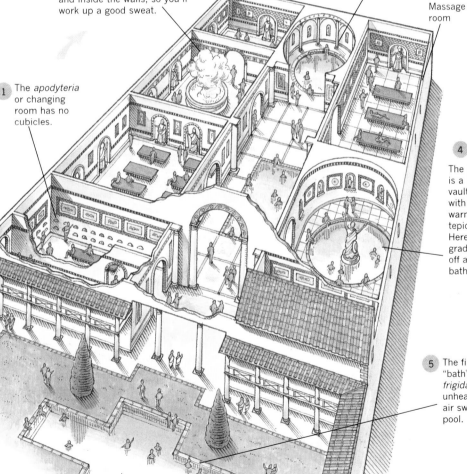

2 The *sudatorium,* or *laconicum,* is a hot air bath like a sauna. Hot air runs under the floor and inside the walls, so you'll work up a good sweat.

3 The *caldarium,* almost as hot as the *laconicum,* has a hot pool. It's often housed in a *rotunda* (a domed-room). This is where you use your *strigil.*

Massage room

1 The *apodyteria* or changing room has no cubicles.

4
The *tepidarium* is a large vaulted hall with a gently-warmed (or tepid) pool. Here, you can gradually cool off as you bathe.

5 The final "bath" is the *frigidarium,* an unheated open-air swimming pool.

WATER PALACES

Top of any tourist's "must-see" list are Trajan's Baths, the biggest Rome has to offer and catering for up to 10,000 people at a time. They've been open for eight years and were inaugurated on June 22nd 109AD, the same day as Trajan's aqueduct, the *Traiana*.

The baths are palatial, with marble walls and pillars, and domed ceilings high above. Many of the ceilings have central holes which let in light. On a bright day, sunlight streams through, heating the rooms.

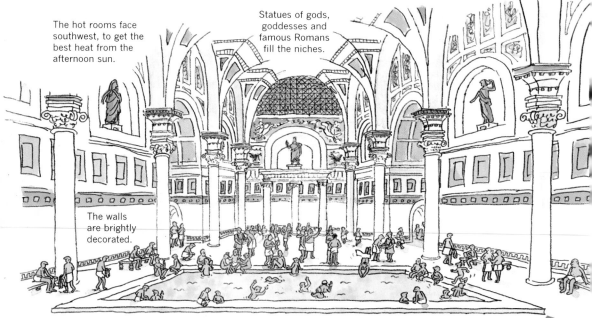

The hot rooms face southwest, to get the best heat from the afternoon sun.

Statues of gods, goddesses and famous Romans fill the niches.

The walls are brightly decorated.

Baths are as much a chance to socialize as to get clean.

The baths took five years to put up, on a giant platform built into the hillside. There are entrances on all sides, but to appreciate their magnificence fully, on your first visit go in through the grand entrance on the north-east side.

Niches filled with amazing statues line every wall. The statue to look out for is the **Laocöon Group**. This magnificent sculpture shows Laocöon, who was the priest of the god Apollo, and his two sons being attacked by serpents.

TOP TIPS FOR TOURISTS
No. 6: The roar of the crowd

Trajan's Baths are certainly the finest, but with anything up to several thousand visitors at a time, they can get very crowded, not to mention noisy. If you prefer to bathe in peace, try the **Baths of Titus** nearby (opposite the Colosseum). They're older and the facilities are less grand, but they're much more restful.

PIPING HOT WATER

In the basement, you can see how the baths are heated. The Romans have invented the *hypocaust*, the first underfloor central heating. But go first thing; it gets unbearably hot. Any later and you'll be dodging fainting slaves, collapsing as they stoke the fires which heat the rooms.

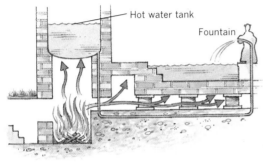

Hot water tank

Fountain

Hot air circulates through tunnels under the baths.

THE TRAJAN CISTERN

It may be a humble cistern (water container), but it's a prime example of Roman engineering. Set into a hill next to the baths, the cistern distributes water to all parts of the bath building. It holds an amazing 8,000,000 l (just over 2,000,000 gals) of water stored on two levels, flowing in from the aqueducts Julia and Claudia.

FUN AND GAMES

Next to cleanliness, in the Roman mind at least, is healthiness, and all baths have gyms and playing grounds attached. Here, you can join in a variety of games, including a form of tennis using your hands instead of a racket.

Games counters and dice for those who prefer less energetic games

Harpastum, named after its sand-filled ball, is a more aggressive ball game. The aim is to get the ball from the other players. Shoving isn't against the rules: it's a good tactic.

Trigon is a game with less contact. Players stand one at each corner of a triangle, throwing balls back and forth at each other without warning. It calls for concentration – you throw and catch simultaneously.

REST AND RELAX!

If running around is just too active for you, don't worry. The baths are surrounded with everything you need for more leisurely pursuits.

A bone comb, a spatula for applying cosmetics, and a tube of cream for beauty treatments after a bath

As well as playing grounds, there are libraries, exhibition halls, covered walkways with fountains, and landscaped gardens. You can have a snack, enjoy a massage, visit a barber, go for a stroll – or all four if the mood takes you. And if being on vacation really takes hold and you feel like a change, you can treat yourself to a Roman makeover by a beautician.

OUT AND ABOUT

As you'd expect in a city of its size, Rome is fast becoming grid-locked. In fact, wheeled vehicles have been banned from the city between dawn and dusk since Caesar's time. This means that most of your visiting will be done on foot.

This wouldn't be a problem if the streets were pleasant places to walk. Certainly, the major streets are swept clean, though they're often unbearably crowded. But in smaller streets and alleys, you'll be up to the ankles in garbage, and even sewage. You'll also be a prime target for any itinerant beggar who happens to cross your path.

The streets are paved though and most sights are fairly close together, so walking isn't such a bad option – as long as you watch your step. You certainly get the feel of the city this way. But be careful crossing roads: the wheels of the night-time traffic wear deep grooves in them, which fill with rainwater.

HIRING A "CAB"

The alternative to pedestrian sightseeing is to hire a litter. This is a wheel-less carriage used by the wealthier citizens and carried by slaves. Choose carefully. They range from the luxurious, with padded cushions, to the dirty, greasy and falling apart.

Being carried in a litter can often prove to be a bumpy ride.

ROMAN UFOs?

Watch out for falling masonry if you decide to walk. The Romans' feats of engineering are second to none, but they also have "cowboy" builders who want a quick profit, no matter how shakily an apartment block is put up.

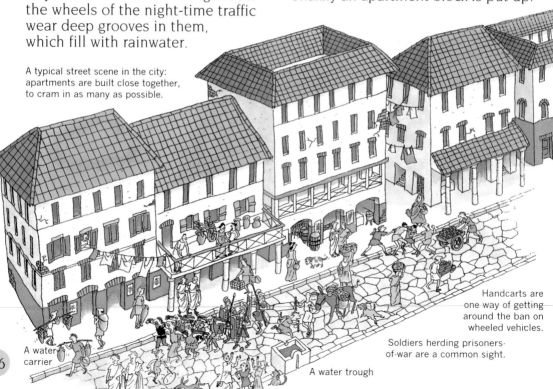

A typical street scene in the city: apartments are built close together, to cram in as many as possible.

Handcarts are one way of getting around the ban on wheeled vehicles.

Soldiers herding prisoners-of-war are a common sight.

A water carrier

A water trough

A ball game

NO-GO AREAS

Even if you want to see the seedier side of Roman life (and it's not all banquets and mosaics), avoid the **Subura** area. It's a slum, the home of Rome's poorest inhabitants and the most disreputable area in Rome. Inevitably, it's become the haunt of thieves, who prey on the unwary.

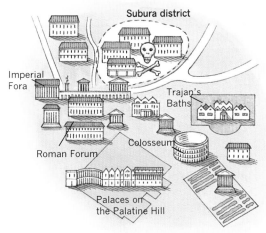

Subura district

Imperial Fora

Trajan's Baths

Roman Forum

Colosseum

Palaces on the Palatine Hill

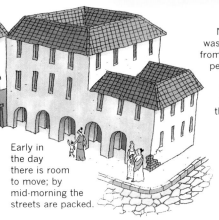

Not only is washing hung from windows, people often throw out household waste too, though this is illegal.

Early in the day there is room to move; by mid-morning the streets are packed.

ROAD SWEEPERS

The *Curatores Viarum* are the people responsible for roads, including street cleaning, garbage disposal and traffic. Complain to them if the streets where you're staying get in too much of a mess.

GETTING LOST

If you do get lost, don't panic. Keep your head and look for a familiar sight with which to orientate yourself. If you should find yourself in the **Subura** district, however, GET OUT AS FAST AS YOU CAN!

TAKE A TORCH

As darkness descends, the already crowded city becomes a nightmare scenario when wheeled vehicles are let in. With no street lighting, most Romans head straight for home. You should too. Hire a torch bearer to guide you safely through the unlit streets. Squads of night watchman patrol the city, but there aren't enough for every part of town.

TOP TIPS FOR TOURISTS
No. 7: Keep a pocket watch

Like all cities, Rome is full of thieves or "cutpurses". If you don't have a money belt, buy a draw-string purse. Hide it in the folds of your toga though, or the strings will be cut, hence the expression "cutpurses".
Hard to come by, but more effective, is a soldier's wrist purse, shown below.

Purses like this can only be opened once they've been taken off.

GETTING SICK

It happens to nearly everyone on vacation, sooner or later: you have an accident or become sick. There's no shortage of Roman options if the worst happens, from chanting to eating dung. But more effective, or at least preferable, is to consult a doctor.

Many doctors work from shops which are open to the road. If you value your privacy, look for one who has rooms in a *domus*. But be warned: there's no formal system of training. Doctors start as apprentices and learn by watching doctors already in practice. There are no qualifications either: in Rome, anyone can call himself a doctor. To be absolutely safe, unless you're desperate, go home for treatment.

REMEDIES

Medicines are made from plants, particularly herbs, and minerals. (There are reputedly as many as 42 remedies made from lettuce alone.) Plants are crushed in a pestle and mortar and made into pills, or added to wine to make a linctus. Doctors don't just prescribe pills though. They're as likely to advise you on the importance of a healthy diet, fresh air and exercise.

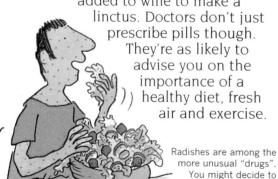

Radishes are among the more unusual "drugs". You might decide to skip the doctor and eat a large salad instead.

MEDICINE AND RELIGION

Although Roman medicine is based to some extent on observation and scientific fact (which comes mainly from the writings of Greek doctors), it's also closely tied up with religion. The causes of disease are barely understood – your doctor is likely to blame your illness on a curse. Most Romans, their doctors included, believe the gods can cure people. A common response to illness is to sleep in the temple of *Aesculapius*, god of medicine, in the hope of dreaming a cure. If a particular part of your body troubles you, leave a small model of it (a *votive*) in the temple. It will remind Aesculapius which part of you needs healing.

A votive eye

66 *I was sick so the Doctor hurried over – with ninety students. Ninety cold hands prodded me. I wasn't well before; now I'm really sick.* 99

Martial (see page 61)

OPTICIANS

The only opticians are actually doctors who specialize in eye complaints. You certainly won't be able to get a sight test, or replace a broken pair of glasses. If you come down with an eye infection though, there are various ointments on offer, and – in extreme cases – even cataract operations are performed.

A hook to hold back wounds during operations

SURGERY

Tweezers

Many doctors are better at surgery than curing illnesses, especially the ones who trained in army hospitals. They have vast experience of anatomy and surgery from treating the wounds of hundreds of soldiers. Operations can be quite complex, from setting broken bones to amputating limbs, though these shouldn't be necessary unless you're very accident-prone.

Surgeons have a wide range of bronze and iron instruments at their disposal, some very delicate. But despite their equipment and expertise, operations are highly dangerous. With no anaesthetics or painkillers, even patients who survive an operation are likely to die of shock or infection soon after.

DENTISTS

If you have a toothache during your stay, you'll be able to find a dentist, but you may not like the treatment. Fillings are unheard of. Instead, your bad teeth will be extracted and false teeth offered in replacement.

Teeth are fixed to a gold band which won't rust.

TOP TIPS FOR TOURISTS
No. 8: No insurance?

Don't panic if money's short and you can't afford consultation fees. A state health system has recently been introduced. Doctors who are part of the scheme aren't taxed on their earnings from richer patients, provided they treat the poorest patients for free.

Herbs are mixed for medicine with a pestle and mortar.

Here, an apprentice medic is given the chance to put his knowledge into practice.

Jugs of wine – the only option for dulling pain

Without X-rays, doctors have to diagnose by feel.

19

THE ROMAN FORUM

There's a forum at the heart of every Roman town. Part market-place, part law court, part religious district, part political arena, it's the place to go for the latest gossip. Each forum usually follows the same basic layout: three covered walkways for offices and shops, making three sides of a square, with the *basilica* or law court forming the fourth. The *curia* (senate house), temples and shrines stand within the square.

The first to be built, however, was the **Roman Forum**, which doesn't follow this pattern. In fact, so many shrines and statues were added, it became too crowded for people to meet. So successive emperors, beginning with Caesar, built their own *fora** – the **Imperial Fora** – alongside (see pages 22-23). But it's in the Roman Forum that you'll really begin to appreciate the majesty and grandeur of Rome.

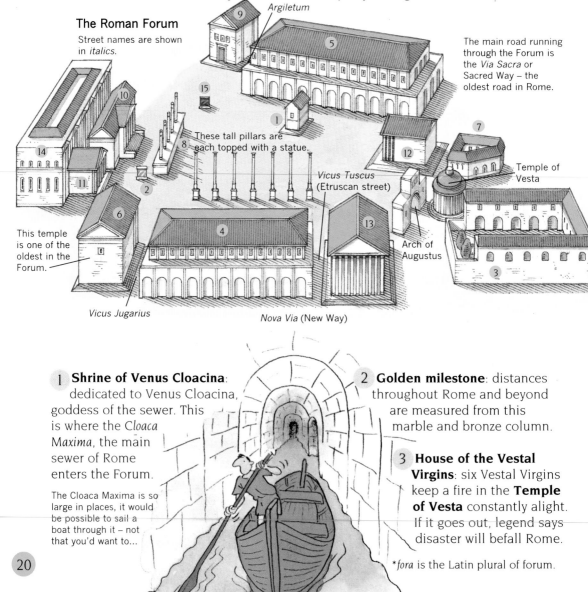

The Roman Forum

Street names are shown in *italics*.

Argiletum

The main road running through the Forum is the *Via Sacra* or Sacred Way – the oldest road in Rome.

These tall pillars are each topped with a statue.

Vicus Tuscus (Etruscan street)

Temple of Vesta

Arch of Augustus

This temple is one of the oldest in the Forum.

Vicus Jugarius

Nova Via (New Way)

1 **Shrine of Venus Cloacina**: dedicated to Venus Cloacina, goddess of the sewer. This is where the *Cloaca Maxima*, the main sewer of Rome enters the Forum.

The Cloaca Maxima is so large in places, it would be possible to sail a boat through it – not that you'd want to...

2 **Golden milestone**: distances throughout Rome and beyond are measured from this marble and bronze column.

3 **House of the Vestal Virgins**: six Vestal Virgins keep a fire in the **Temple of Vesta** constantly alight. If it goes out, legend says disaster will befall Rome.

**fora* is the Latin plural of forum.

Lawyers hire crowds to cheer them on and boo their opponents, so trials can get rowdy.

4 **Basilica Julia**: a court house, begun by Julius Caesar, the Republican dictator, in around 55BC. 180 magistrates try cases here. If you have a spare half hour, sit in on a trial in the public gallery upstairs.

5 **Basilica Aemilia**: the second *basilica* or law court to be built in Rome, it was put up in 179BC.

6 **Temple of Saturn**: the first temple to the god Saturn on this site dates back to the beginning of the Republic*, some 500-600 years ago. Saturn was said to have taught the Romans how to farm.

In December, the lively festival of Saturnalia is held. Masters and slaves switch places for the day and gifts are exchanged.

7 **Regia**: the official headquarters of the chief priest of Rome.

8 **Rostra**: the large stone platform initially used by public speakers to rouse the crowds. Now it's mostly used for official ceremonies. The name comes from the ships' *rostra* (prows) which decorate it.

9 **Curia** (Senate House): during the Republic, senators met here to govern Rome. Before each session, the President would consult an *augur* (someone who interprets messages from the gods). Though they still meet, senators now have little sway: emperors are all-powerful.

An *augur*, usually a senator, is a highly respected religious figure.

* see page 59

10 **Temple of Concord** (Peace): built to celebrate the peace between warring factions in Rome in the third century BC.

11 **Temple of Vespasian**: a temple built in memory of the emperor Vespasian. (Emperors become gods after they die.)

12 **Temple of Caesar**: dedicated to Julius Caesar and built on the spot where his body was cremated. Inside, is a statue of Caesar with a star on his head. This is because a comet appeared during the weeks of shows given by Augustus in Caesar's memory.

Many people believe the comet was Caesar's soul going up to heaven.

13 **Temple of Castor**: dedicated to the god Jupiter's twin sons, Castor and Pollux, who are said to have helped the Romans in battle.

14 **Tabularium**: the public record office, where state records are kept.

15 **Lapis Niger** (Black stone): a slab of black marble which some say marks the grave of Romulus, founder of Rome. Others think it is the site of an old temple to the god Vulcan.

21

THE IMPERIAL FORA

The first of the five **Imperial Fora** was begun by Caesar in 51BC, when the Roman Forum became too small to hold the crowds who gathered to discuss politics, attend court or simply to trade. Augustus, Vespasian, Nerva and Trajan then added their *fora* alongside. Like the original, all contain law courts, shops, markets and temples.

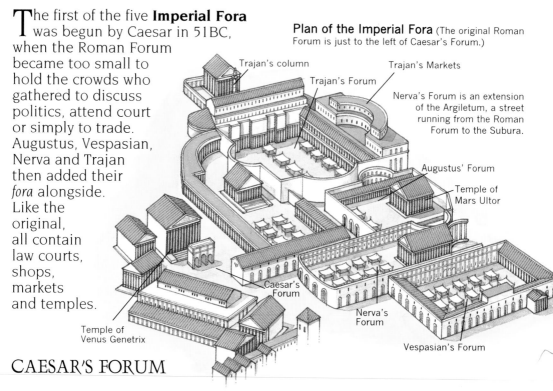

Plan of the Imperial Fora (The original Roman Forum is just to the left of Caesar's Forum.)

Trajan's column

Trajan's Forum

Trajan's Markets

Nerva's Forum is an extension of the Argiletum, a street running from the Roman Forum to the Subura.

Augustus' Forum

Temple of Mars Ultor

Caesar's Forum

Nerva's Forum

Vespasian's Forum

Temple of Venus Genetrix

CAESAR'S FORUM

To make room for his forum, Caesar had to buy and demolish an entire street of houses which stood in the way. Costs are estimated at between 60 million and 100 million *sestertii*. You can judge for yourself whether it was worth it. Caesar's Forum was partly damaged in a fire in AD80, but Domitian began restoration work, which Trajan has just completed.

You can reach **Caesar's Forum** via the Curia in the Roman Forum. Dominating the scene is the **Temple of Venus Genitrix**, from whom Caesar claimed he was descended.

In front of the temple is a statue of Caesar on his horse, displaying its unusual hooves. (Soothsayers are said to have told Caesar that the split hooves were a sign from the gods that he would rule the world.) Inside is a statue of Venus, based on the Egyptian queen, Cleopatra.

Close by is the **Tullianum**, a prison which houses enemies of the state. It consists of two underground rooms, cut out of the Capitoline Hill. Legend has it that Saint Peter and Saint Paul were imprisoned here.

Saint Peter is said to have made water flow from the earth to baptize guards and inmates.

FORA GALORE

Vespasian's Forum is also known as the Peace Forum. A Temple of Peace was built here in AD71, after the Jews were defeated in a war in Judea (Palestine).

Augustus' Forum stretches from the Roman Forum up to a slum district. The back wall is high, to keep the forum apart from the hovels behind it, and to protect it from the frequent fires which rage through them. This forum has the **Temple of Mars Ultor**, which is now a museum for relics, including Caesar's sword.

Trajan's Forum is overlooked by his magnificent markets (see pages 40-41) and consists of a *basilica*, a temple, and a courtyard with two libraries, one on either side of his famous column.

TRAJAN'S COLUMN

Trajan's Column, 38m (125ft) high, is made up of marble panels going up in a spiral. The panels show episodes from wars Trajan waged – over 100 scenes are illustrated. As the column goes higher, its width increases, so it doesn't look as if it narrows at the top. The panels are larger too. In a chamber at the base is a golden urn containing the ashes of Trajan and his wife – the only Romans allowed to be buried within the city.

TOP TIPS FOR TOURISTS
No. 9: Trajan's Column

For the best view of this stunning sculpture, head for the roof-top terrace on one of the Forum's libraries.

A detail from Trajan's column showing shipbuilders at work

THE COLOSSEUM

In future centuries, the **Colosseum** stadium will be famous worldwide, but ask for it in Rome and you'll receive blank stares. It's still called the **Flavian Amphitheatre**, after the family who had it built. It won't get the name Colosseum until Hadrian has the statue of Nero, known as the Colossus, moved beside it from its present site by Trajan's Baths.

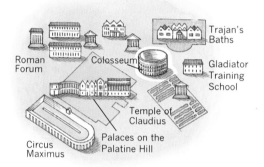

Roman Forum
Colosseum
Trajan's Baths
Gladiator Training School
Temple of Claudius
Circus Maximus
Palaces on the Palatine Hill

THE BUILDING

Whatever you call it, the Colosseum is a stunning arena for "the Games" – spectacular (but bloodthirsty) shows. Seating 50,000, it's divided into three:

A **The arena**: the name comes from the *harena* (sand) spread on the floor. Underneath runs a network of passages, storing scenery, cages for wild animals, and mechanisms to hoist them to the surface.

B **The podium**: a broad terrace on top of the arena wall. The best spot is reserved for the Emperor; remaining seats are taken by senators and foreign ambassadors.

C **The cavea**: this is divided into three tiers of seats separated by landings, reached by staircases and 160 passages.

GETTING IN AND OUT

There are 80 entrance arches, all numbered except for the four main entrances. Free tickets are given out early in the morning. Each ticket has a number which matches an arch. You enter through the arch with the same number as your ticket.

Only men are allowed in the first two tiers of the *cavea*. Women must sit above them, separated by a wall. Behind the women, against the outer wall, is standing room for slaves. Don't let the number of people overwhelm you. The building can be evacuated in ten minutes.

The *velarium* is a vast sunshade, like a sail, which is dragged across the top of the arena using ropes and pulleys.

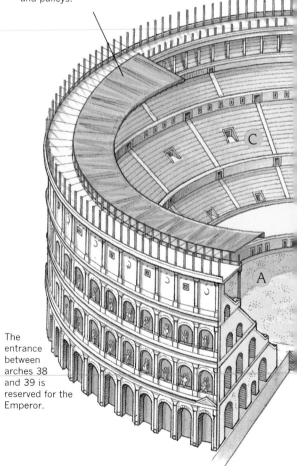

The entrance between arches 38 and 39 is reserved for the Emperor.

THE SHOW

If you're determined to risk a visit, it's not all bad, though the bad is horrific. Usually, the performance opens with a procession and pantomime show. This often includes conjurors, though you'll probably be too high up to appreciate them. There are also circus acts – panthers pulling chariots and elephants tracing Latin phrases in the sand with their trunks. But if this sounds too much like animal cruelty to you, don't hang around.

The high wall around the arena is to protect the audience from the animals.

B

The Imperial box

The Colosseum has a circumference of 527m (1,730ft) and is 57m (187ft) tall. The arena measures 76 x 46m (249 x 151ft).

The building is made of a white stone called travertine, brought in from quarries outside Rome.

GLADIATORS

The Colosseum is known for its battles to the death between men, women and animals. Victims are criminals and prisoners-of-war, but Rome also has hundreds of fighting professionals called gladiators. Many are slaves given the chance to go to training school where they learn to fight. A few become rich and famous; most die young. Below are five types:

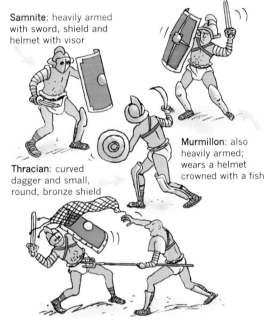

Samnite: heavily armed with sword, shield and helmet with visor

Thracian: curved dagger and small, round, bronze shield

Murmillon: also heavily armed; wears a helmet crowned with a fish

Secutor – "pursuer": fights Retarius with sword; wears helmet, shield, leg guards and protection on sword arm

Retarius – "net fighter": fights with a net and trident; has one arm protected

WARNING!

The shows – wholesale slaughter in the name of entertainment – are not for the squeamish. You may prefer to admire the building from the outside alone. Rome is more than guts and gore, though you could be forgiven for forgetting it at the Colosseum.

CHARIOT RACING

If you want to rest your feet (though not your lungs), see a sporting event and spend a day at the races. Chariot racing is one of the most popular spectator sports in Rome. It's certainly less violent than the Games, though it is dangerous and accidents are common.

GOING TO THE RACES

Races take place at "circuses": purpose-built buildings which house the racetracks. There are five or six in Rome, but the oldest and most famous is the **Circus Maximus**. It's the largest in the empire, seating up to 250,000 people. The stadium starts filling up at dawn, so set out early or hire someone to save you a seat. As there's no entry fee, it's worth it. Men should wear togas: the races are only for citizens and their families.

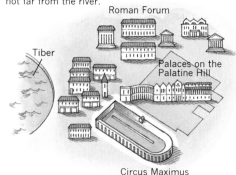

The Circus Maximus stands in front of the palaces on the Palatine Hill not far from the river.

Roman Forum

Tiber

Palaces on the Palatine Hill

Circus Maximus

At the entrance, there are three arcades decorated with marble. Here you'll find wine sellers and pastry cooks. It's a good idea to stock up on refreshments before you go in, or you'll spend the day fighting your way through crowds rather than watching the races.

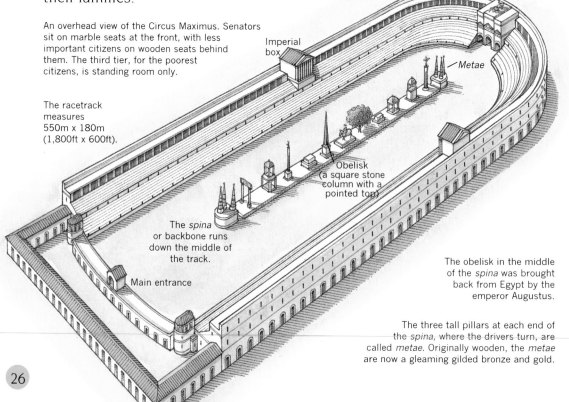

An overhead view of the Circus Maximus. Senators sit on marble seats at the front, with less important citizens on wooden seats behind them. The third tier, for the poorest citizens, is standing room only.

Imperial box

Metae

The racetrack measures 550m x 180m (1,800ft x 600ft).

Obelisk (a square stone column with a pointed top)

The *spina* or backbone runs down the middle of the track.

Main entrance

The obelisk in the middle of the *spina* was brought back from Egypt by the emperor Augustus.

The three tall pillars at each end of the *spina*, where the drivers turn, are called *metae*. Originally wooden, the *metae* are now a gleaming gilded bronze and gold.

TOP TIPS FOR TOURISTS
No. 10: Fanatical fans

Whatever happens, DON'T get carried away with excitement and cheer your team, "Come on you Reds!" if you're in a crowd of another team's supporters. Fans support their teams with a passion and it won't go down well. Remember: some Romans look upon a violent brawl as just another part of a fun day out.

BEFORE THE RACE

Like many events here, the spectacle begins with a procession. First, a band leads on the dignitary, often a consul, who is to start the races. He's accompanied by his attendants, who are followed by singers, and priests carrying images of the gods. All this happens to tremendous applause.

The excitement reaches fever-pitch if the Emperor attends to start the races and takes his place in the box overlooking the finishing line. You'll feel the tension mount as the white cloth, which signals the start of each race, is raised and dropped. The twelve gates at the start line open and the drivers charge out on their chariots, going counter-clockwise around the track.

"... AND THEY'RE OFF!"

Each race – and there are 24 a day – lasts seven laps and covers about eight kms (six miles). There can be up to 12 drivers in a race, racing for one of four teams: the Blues, the Reds, the Greens or the Whites. You'll see races for two, three or four-horse chariots. The more horses, the harder the chariot is to control.

As each lap is completed, a marker in the form of a golden egg or dolphin is turned on a rack on the *spina*.

Things get dangerous as drivers jostle for position, when rounding the bend at each end of the track. If a driver falls, it's onto sand, but he has to be quick to leap out of the way of the other chariots thundering past. The race winner receives a palm leaf of victory, a purse of gold and instant fame. Even horses can become celebrities in their own right.

Drivers wrap the reins around their waists. Each driver carries a knife to cut himself free if his chariot overturns.

27

SEEING A PLAY

A less grisly outing than the Games, though not always by much, is a trip to see a play. Even if you're not that interested in Greek or Roman drama, it's worth a visit for the buildings alone.

A curtain is raised in front of the stage for scenery changes.

This stage is made of stone, unlike the earliest versions, which were wooden and temporary.

Changing rooms for the actors are on either side of the stage.

Seats are allocated according to status: the rich (as ever) at the front.

> **66** If you're going to a play, take plenty of cushions. The stone seats are uncomfortable to sit on for more than half an hour. **99**
>
> A numb-bottomed drama fan

The **Theatrum Pompei** (built for Pompey), which holds 27,000 people, was the first to be built of stone, in 55BC. Handier for the sightseer, though, is the **Theatrum Marcelli** (built for Marcellus), which stands alongside the **Circus Maximus**.

TOP TIPS FOR TOURISTS
No. 11: 'Tis the season

Choose the dates of your visit carefully if you want to see a play. They're only performed between April and November, and then only on certain days.

AUDIENCE REACTION

At home, you may be used to watching plays in respectful silence. Not so here. The audience gets very involved, screaming, booing and hissing as the play progresses. It's not uncommon for riots to break out in the middle of a performance, as people debate the merits of the different actors.

PLAY OR PANTOMIME?

Don't be misled by the grand buildings. Plays don't always live up to the elegance of their surroundings. This is partly because of size: the **Theatrum Marcelli** (built for Marcellus), seats 14,000. Such a vast, open-air performance area is not the place for subtlety.

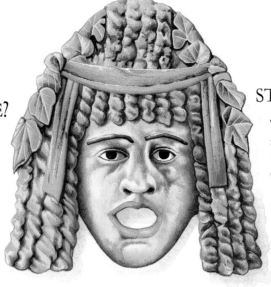

Masks are painted to look natural, but in bold shades to stand out.

In fact, recent years have seen a dramatic change in the style of plays. Large crowds, remote from the action on stage, cannot follow complicated plots. So, speeches have been cut and plays reduced to a chorus singing songs, with actors miming the action. Bawdy comedies are the most popular, though a new and brutal realism sometimes creeps in, as actors try to outdo the Games for blood and gore.

STEREOTYPES

To make plays simple and easily understood, characters are reduced to stereotypes, such as "wise old man" or "smiling fool". The actors' faces can't be seen from high up, so they wear masks with strong expressions. Masks are often dark or pale, to indicate whether the character is male or female. Behind the masks, though, all actors are male.

MIME

Mime is becoming increasingly popular and, here, none of the usual conventions apply. The actors wear normal clothes, there are no masks – and even women are allowed to take part. The emphasis is still on realism, though. You may find some shows too realistic for comfort.

KEY TO COSTUMES

Actors' robes are designed to show who they are playing:

Red robes signify a poor person.

Slave characters wear plain tunics.

Purple robes indicate a rich citizen.

The costumes of elderly characters tend to be white.

Actors portraying young characters will wear several shades.

ARCHITECTURAL ART

Roman architecture, decoratively at least, borrows heavily from the Greeks. But the Romans' real interest in architecture is a far more practical one. They need massive aqueducts to carry vast supplies of water, and large arenas to cope with an ever-expanding viewing public. It is these requirements, combined with innovations in engineering, which have resulted in some spectacular pieces of architecture.

SPOTTER'S GUIDE TO COLUMNS

Columns are everywhere in Greek and therefore Roman architecture. If you like looking out for things while you're sightseeing, keep this page open and see how many of each column you can spot. Three – the Corinthian, Ionic and Doric – are based on Greek designs. The Composite is a combination of the Corinthian and Ionic columns, while the Tuscan is all Roman.

The five columns used in Roman buildings are shown below. At one end of the scale, Corinthian columns are used for temples and palaces.

ARCHES

Arches were introduced by the Etruscans, but the Romans have developed their use into a fine art. Before the Romans, most buildings were topped off with a beam of wood or stone. The invention of the arch means builders can now span much greater distances.

VAULTS

A cutaway diagram to show cross-vaulting (see below)

Often dismissed as architectural copycats, the Romans have some great inventions to their name, including tunnel vaults – arches placed side by side to form a tunnel. From tunnel vaults came cross vaulting: two tunnel vaults meeting at right angles to each other.

DOMES

But perhaps most spectacular of all is another invention created from arches: the dome. This is made by crossing lots of arches over each other, to enclose a circular area.

1 CORINTHIAN

The much plainer Tuscan columns are used for army camps and prisons.

2 IONIC

3 COMPOSITE

4 DORIC

5 TUSCAN

THE PANTHEON

The **Pantheon**, currently being rebuilt under Hadrian, is planned to have the largest dome in existence. Also known as the "Temple to all the gods", it will be the city's most stunning monument when finished.

Like most Roman temples, the original Pantheon was based on a Greek design. Hadrian's will retain the same style for the *portico*, or porch. Past the entrance, though, all similarity to Greek temples will end.

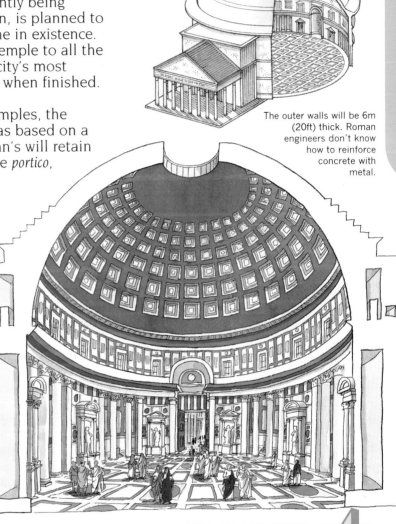

The opening will measure a vast 8.8m (30ft) across, a daring feat of engineering.

The outer walls will be 6m (20ft) thick. Roman engineers don't know how to reinforce concrete with metal.

An artist's impression of how the Pantheon will look when finished:

Inside and out, the roof will be covered with sheets of bronze.

The squares in the roof are *coffers*, made from blocks of wood which will support the dome until the concrete sets.

Heavy concrete will be used at the base of the dome, then lighter materials higher up.

Seven alcoves are to be set in the walls, each to hold a giant statue of a god.

From the outside, the Pantheon will be impressive enough. But inside, the hall's sheer size and the magical quality of the light will take your breath away. An *oculus* (circular opening) in the roof will let sunlight stream through (not to mention rain if it's wet). Visitors who stay a while, will see the light move around the dome as the earth turns.

TOP TIPS FOR TOURISTS
No. 12: A building site

To see the construction in progress, pop along to the site. There are no barriers to keep you out but take care – there won't be any hard hats on offer.

MILITARY PROCESSIONS

All roads may lead to Rome, but inside the city, the most famous is the **Via Sacra** (Sacred Way). Pick a spot along it to see military processions, as they pass by on their way to the **Capitoline Hill**, to give thanks for victory. Such displays not only celebrate success in battle, they're the perfect way to emphasize the power and grandeur of Rome.

A military procession will surely be one of the most stirring sights you'll encounter during your visit.

MARCHING ORDERS

At the head of the procession are the magistrates and senators, the leaders of Rome. They're followed by the spoils of war – the treasures and prisoners taken from the defeated enemy, sometimes carried on litters for the crowd to see.

Then come the soldiers, their uniforms gleaming, and wagons with people enacting key episodes from the campaign. Look out for the General and, more particularly, the slave standing behind him in the chariot.

A wreath of laurel leaves, worn by emperors instead of a crown

The slave will be holding a wreath over the General's head. As the General acknowledges the cheers of the crowd, the slave is constantly whispering in his ear, "Remember you are but mortal." (He wouldn't say that to the Emperor!)

A standard

The General

Each legion* has its own standard. With every successful campaign, another symbol is added to it.

A soldier called the *Aquilifer* walks near the head of the procession, wearing a lion skin. He carries the standard of his century*, topped with an eagle.

*A century is a group of 80 soldiers; a legion is made up of around 5,000 men: see pages 54-55.

TRIUMPHAL ARCHES

Arches have sprung up all over Rome, as successive emperors commemorate their victories. Of these, the carvings on **Trajan's Arch**, which stands on the **Via Appia**, are especially worth seeing.

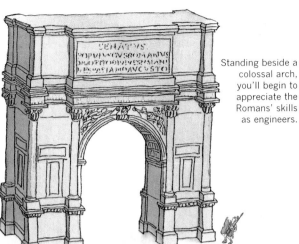

Standing beside a colossal arch, you'll begin to appreciate the Romans' skills as engineers.

TITUS

The **Arch of Titus**, situated close to the **Temple of Venus and Rome**, spans the *Via Sacra* as it runs between the Colosseum and the Forum. It was built to celebrate Titus' victory at the fall of Jerusalem in AD70 – the culmination of a campaign his father Vespasian had waged for the previous four years. The arch is built entirely of marble and was only completed after Titus' early death.

On the arch are some of the most spectacular sculptures of any arch in Rome, including Titus triumphant in his chariot, and a procession displaying the treasures pillaged from the temple in Jerusalem.

Below is a detail from the Arch of Titus, showing the victorious procession with captured loot. This detail is found on the inside of the arch.

TOP TIPS FOR TOURISTS
No. 13: Watch your language

If your Latin is up to it, in among the cheers you may hear the odd insult being hurled at the generals. It's considered good luck, but *only* when shouted by soldiers. Don't try it yourself or your luck will swiftly change...

DOLABELLA

The **Arch of Dolabella**, which stands at the end of the *Via Claudia*, carries **Nero's Aqueduct** which supplies water to the Palatine Hill.

AUGUSTUS

Between the temples of **Castor** and **Caesar** in the Roman Forum, look for the **Arch of Augustus**, built to celebrate Augustus' victory over Mark Antony, a Roman consul, and the Queen of Egypt, Cleopatra.

TOMBS AND CATACOMBS

Aside from military processions, you'll probably see at least one important funeral procession during your stay too. The mortality rate is high, especially for children, and few people live beyond 50.

Funerals are a chance for a family to show off its wealth and status. As such, they can be very elaborate. Don't be surprised to see the body itself. It's carried on an open litter, sometimes posed sitting up, so that everyone can see who has died.

First, the body is washed and covered in oil. If the person was a senator, he is dressed in his official robes. Then the body is covered in flowers and wreaths, before lying on display for several days, for visitors to pay their last respects.

On the day of the funeral, the procession heads first to the forum where a speech is made praising the person, before he is buried outside the city. With space at a premium inside, the law requires that all graves are outside the city walls.

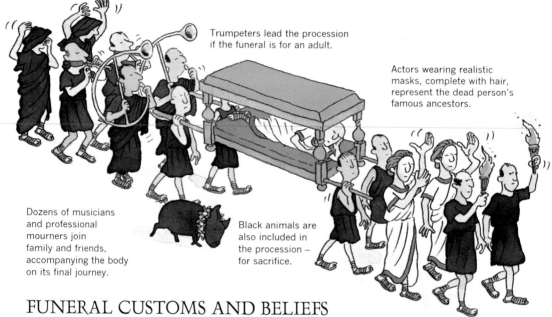

Trumpeters lead the procession if the funeral is for an adult.

Actors wearing realistic masks, complete with hair, represent the dead person's famous ancestors.

Dozens of musicians and professional mourners join family and friends, accompanying the body on its final journey.

Black animals are also included in the procession – for sacrifice.

FUNERAL CUSTOMS AND BELIEFS

The dead person is dressed in his finest clothes, with a coin placed under his tongue. The Romans believe that after death a person is ferried to the underworld, or Hades, across the river Styx. The coin is to pay the ferryman.

It's put into the person's mouth as their hands are often filled with cakes to feed Cerberus, the three-headed dog who guards Hades. On arrival in the underworld, a person's spirit is judged and sent either to *Elysium* (heaven) or *Tantarus* (hell).

COLOSSEUM

THE APPIAN WAY

Many tombs lie along the **Appian Way**, or *Via Appia*, the main road leading out of Rome to the south.

A journey along the Appian Way makes for an interesting excursion. Most of the tombs are grand affairs and you can learn a great deal about Roman life from reading people's histories on their tombs.

You can pick up a litter or a carriage from the stables at one of the gates leading out of the city. There's no system of inspections though, and not all stables are reputable, so check your horse before you ride.

Tombs often have elaborate carvings which show an aspect of the dead person's life.

The Appian Way is 122 miles (196 kms) long and sees a constant stream of traffic.

OSTIA

CATACOMBS

Traditionally, funerals ended with a cremation, though burials have recently come into fashion. For a more gruesome trip, visit a *columbarium* – an underground chamber or catacomb, filled with urns holding the ashes of cremated Romans. Be careful: catacombs are used by outlawed groups, such as Christians, to meet secretly. If you come across such a group, leave quickly or you risk arrest.

TOP TIPS FOR TOURISTS
No. 14: Crocodile tears

The Romans hire professional mourners, called *praeficae*, to grieve at their funerals. It's a job you might consider if your money runs out. You'll be given a tear bottle in which to catch your tears. But don't spill any – mourners are paid by the amount they shed. To make sure the tears flow, you might find it helps to go via a market to pick up a raw onion.

A tear bottle

35

DAY-TO-DAY SHOPPING

Whether you're looking for souvenirs of your stay or something for supper, Rome has shops and markets to suit every taste, not to mention each purse. The more exclusive shops, and markets for fresh produce, are found in the *fora* (see pages 20-23), but the shops for everyday goods are housed on the ground floors of apartments.

Most have a counter across the front, over which you choose and buy the goods. You'll find everything from bacon to pots and pans, oil lamps and cloth. Not everyone can afford the luxury of a shop. Many people offer their goods or services from portable stalls set up by the road.

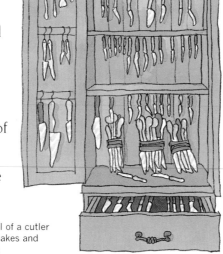

The portable stall of a cutler (someone who makes and sharpens knives)

CRAFTSMEN AT WORK

Virtually everything that has to be manufactured – bread from flour, for example, or tables and chairs from timber – is made on the premises. So, even if there's nothing you need, you can enjoy the spectacle of goods being produced right in front of you.

Craftsmen in the shops along the street might not sell goods of the quality of those found in a forum, but they're equally fascinating to watch. Even making the most mundane cookware requires a skilled potter, and you can easily spend half an hour watching one cast dishes and plates on his wheel.

A view of a street from the back of shops. The shoppers are mostly slaves, for whom shopping is a daily chore.

TOP TIPS FOR TOURISTS
No. 15: Eco packaging

Rome is a truly eco-friendly city when it comes to packaging – shopkeepers just don't use any. Everything is sold unwrapped, so bring a basket from home or buy one before you shop. For oil or wine, you'll need to bring your own bottles or jugs.

Metalworkers making household tools

Oil lamps are the only form of artificial light apart from candles.

FAST FOOD

Peer into the back of any bakery you pass and you'll see slaves working a large stone mill, to grind flour. With bread baking in stone ovens as you watch – and smell – you'll find it hard to resist.

If you'd like to drizzle olive oil on your hot-from-the-oven purchase, visit one of the numerous olive oil shops. Many have their own presses to squeeze the oil from the fruit. The oil is stored in large jars called *amphorae* which are lowered into the ground to keep cool.

NEW SHOES

Having pounded the streets sightseeing, you may need a new pair of sandals. These too are made on the spot. Visit a shoemaker, who will make a pair to your measurements.

A pair of hand-made sandals

OPENING HOURS

With poor artificial light, Romans make the most of daylight hours. Since all deliveries must be made before dawn anyway, shops open early. They close at noon for the hottest part of the day, when you'd be advised to follow the Roman lead and have a siesta. Shops reopen in the afternoon and shut at dusk.

> " *Aching feet? Visit a pharmacist. They have a wide selection of herbal ointments and potions, including those to soothe the sole! And if they fail, you can always ask for a magic spell. But be warned. They're not cheap and I've never found one which worked.* "
>
> *A foot-sore shopper*

An oil shop – oil is used for cooking, washing and lighting.

An amphora

In this bakery, slaves are working the mill but it's not unusual to see a donkey turning it.

An olive press

A SHOPPER'S PARADISE

For the ritzier and most exclusive boutiques, head upmarket to one of the *fora*. As a rule of thumb, the closer you get to any forum, the more fashionable the shops become, selling more exotic items (in Roman eyes at least), such as books and fine cloth. Prices are expensive but generally not outrageous. If you can't afford them, you can at least enjoy browsing with senators and their wives.

SPECIALIST STREETS

Of all the streets in Rome the **Vicus Tuscus** is probably the best-known for shopping. It's named after the Etruscan merchants who own most of the shops. Here, you'll find the finest silks, imported from the Greek island of Cos. Close by are specialist perfumiers, who will make you up a scent from your choice of fragrances, not to mention shops selling cosmetics and highly decorated and polished, silver mirrors.

A perfume bottle

THE ORIGINAL KEYRING

One very useful souvenir is a lockable casket for valuables. It comes with a key designed to be worn as a ring.

Key-rings are made of iron, rather than silver or gold which would be too soft.

GLASSWARE

One item you may wish to buy in the forum – it's a little cheaper than gold or silver – is glassware. Glass has become fashionable in wealthy households, as you'll see from the quality and choice on offer. (Poorer households make do with pottery cups and jugs.) Available glass varies from the almost (but not entirely) transparent to opaque.

Glassblowers heat the glass in ovens shaped like beehives.

COLLECTABLES

With the Romans' admiration for Greek art, there's a current craze for all things Greek. You can't move for the antique Greek vases and statues everywhere. All of Rome is collecting them, from the Emperor down, so you're bound to find something in your price range. If you're on a spending spree, you could consider an Etruscan bronze or a citrus wood table. They're very expensive, though, and less transportable than a vase.

Be careful! That statue impulse buy could prove difficult to take home.

JEWELS AND BANGLES

Along the south side of the **Basilica Aemilia**, in the **Roman Forum**, are shops belonging to the gold and silversmiths. They make exquisite bracelets, brooches, necklaces, rings and tiaras, all with fantastic designs. You'll notice well-off Roman women go overboard, positively draping themselves in the stuff.

A necklace of solid gold and a cameo brooch. The bracelet, of a snake, is worn on the upper arm.

> *If you can afford a gold bracelet, ask for it to be engraved with a good luck message. But if you want it in any language other than Latin, you'll have to write it down.*
>
> A poor but happy visitor

BOOKS

For books, head to the **Argiletum**, which runs alongside the **Basilica Aemilia**. Watching a bookshop owner's 20 odd slaves laboriously copying out a book for sale, you'll realize why books are so rare and expensive. Since they also rely on the accuracy of the copyists, no two copies of one book are the same.

Books are made of sheets of papyrus stuck together (see page 53).

People are hired to read manuscripts aloud to scribes, who each take down a copy.

COSMETICS

Wealthy Roman women have a personal make-up artist, an *ornatrix*, to make them up each day. Even if you can't afford that, you might like to buy some Roman cosmetics. There's a wide selection, all made from natural, if strange, ingredients, such as wood ash and red wine.

TOP TIPS FOR TOURISTS
No. 16: Caveat emptor

When shopping, bear in mind the Roman phrase (still used in the 20th century): *Caveat emptor*! ("Buyer Beware!") and check goods carefully before you pay for them.

MARKETS

At the other end of the scale from the exclusive shops in the forum are the market stalls. The markets are set up in the central areas of *fora* and found all over the city.

Some specialize in just one product and these generally open one day a week. Others are open daily, and sell a whole variety of things. You'll find cabbages and beans alongside stalls selling woollen cloth or earthenware jugs.

TRAJAN'S MARKET

The markets in the **Imperial Fora** are close together, a bonus if you like to compare prices of goods before buying (see the plan on page 22). But if you only go to one, make it **Trajan's Market**, overlooking his forum. Despite its name, this is no mere collection of stalls, but 150 shops and offices on terraces. Fruit and flowers are sold on the lower levels, with oil, vinegar and imported items higher up. Don't miss the fifth floor, with its fantastic view, and fishponds where you can buy fish so fresh they're still swimming.

Trajan's Market

Offices on the upper levels are used to hand out free corn to Rome's unemployed.

The shops and offices are ranged on terraces over five floors.

Shops on the ground floor are smaller and cooler than those above.

TOP TIPS FOR TOURISTS
No. 17: An early start

If you want the freshest produce, try to be at the market as it opens – your fellow shoppers, mostly slaves, will be up well before dawn.

FARM FRESH

A huge variety of produce is brought in daily from farms outside the city. Don't expect to buy potatoes, peppers or tomatoes though – or chocolate. They come from Central America which has no trading links with Rome. In fact, the Romans don't even know the American continent exists.

Market stall traders only sell organic produce, as Roman farmers don't use pesticides. (They have no choice – pesticides haven't been invented yet.)

A slave auction taking place: slaves wear signs around their necks advertising their skills. Most are prisoners of war.

A FAIR DEAL

To ensure you aren't cheated, government inspectors called *aediles* make regular visits to the markets, checking both the quality of goods on sale and testing the weights and measures for accuracy.

Your goods will either be weighed on a simple balance, or a device called a steelyard. Various amounts are marked off along the bar. The stallholder moves the weight along it, until the scale balances.

A steelyard

Weights can be intricately carved, often portraying the heads of famous emperors and generals.

SLAVE AUCTION

One of the most commonly traded commodities, after food and wine, is people. This will prove something of a culture shock to many visitors. Though it is offensive to tourists from later times, Romans accept the practice without question.

Slaves are bought like any other property and sold off to the highest bidder. Their subsequent treatment depends wholly on the kindness or otherwise of their master. Not all slaves become menial servants however. Many, in particular those from Greece, find work as doctors, tutors or librarians.

❝❝ *The flower stalls are amazing, with hundreds of brilliant blooms. You can't miss them: they're next to the fish stalls, in an attempt to hide the smell. Buy huge bunches of the cheapest flowers, to freshen up a stuffy apartment.* ❞❞

A tourist who missed air freshener

THE PORT OF ROME

If you want to see where all the goods you've bought enter the city, visit the **Port of Rome** just downstream from the **Theatrum Marcelli**. You can easily spend a pleasant hour or two, watching barges being pulled up the **Tiber**.

The Port of Rome

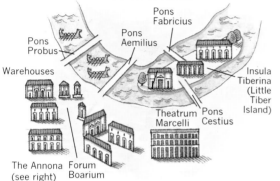

ON THE WHARF

Along the banks of the Tiber, you'll see the gigantic warehouses, or *horrea*, where the barges are unloaded. Some specialize in only one product, such as pepper or spices. You can tell the latter by the fragrant smells which linger in the air. Others are general stores, hoarding wine, oil, marble, cloth, timber, wool, tiles – the list is almost endless. Keep an eye out for flying pottery as you walk around. Jars which have contained olive oil can't be reused, so they're smashed on the quay and used as ballast to weigh down ships.

The barges set out from the sea port of **Ostia**, some 25kms (15 miles) outside the city. Cargoes from merchant ships are unloaded onto barges at Ostia, for the final leg of the journey to Rome. Barges moor by the **Pons Aemilius**, which dates back to the second century BC and was the first bridge to span the river.

Olive oil jars being shattered at the dockside.

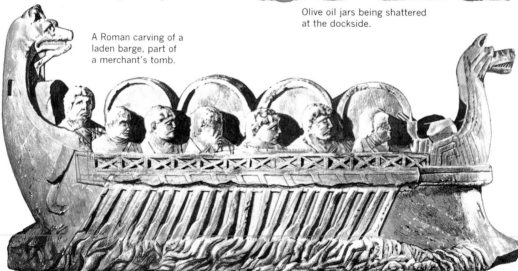

A Roman carving of a laden barge, part of a merchant's tomb.

**No. 18: Insula Tiberina
(Little Tiber Island)**

Look out for the small island
in the middle of the Tiber,
reached by the bridges *Pons
Fabricius* and *Pons Cestius* (see
map on left). It has been
landscaped to look like a boat.
At the front end is a temple to
Aesculapius, god of medicine.

THE ANNONA

The **Annona** is the massive state
warehouse where free corn for
Rome's unemployed is stored and
distributed. At least a third of
Rome's population depends on free
corn for survival. Men line up for a
wooden tablet to prove their
family's entitlement. But three
groups of people are ineligible:
soldiers, slaves, and visitors
passing through the city, so don't
be tempted to join the line.

Goods stored in warehouses
are sold to traders
and the general
public.

WHOLESALE MARKETS

To see where shopkeepers buy their
supplies, and gain an insight into
the sheer scale of Roman trade,
visit the Forum Holitorium and the
Forum Boarium. They're right next
to the Port of Rome.

The **Forum Holitorium**, which sells
fruit and vegetables, lies at the foot
of the Capitoline Hill.

The **Forum Boarium** is the cattle
and poultry market. It's situated
beside the Annona, facing the Tiber,
with temples in among the livestock.

There are round temples to
Hercules and Portunus, the
god of rivers and ports,
in the cattle market.

HERCULES AND THE COWS

*Legend says that Hercules drove
cattle through the Forum Boarium.
He rested by the Tiber where Cacus,
a three-headed, fire-breathing
monster, tried to steal some cows.
Cacus hoped to avoid detection by
making them walk facing the wrong
way. But Hercules saw through the
trick and slew him on the spot.*

OSTIA

Ostia is well worth a couple of days' visit if you're thinking of venturing out of the city. The main seaport of Rome, it stands at the mouth of the Tiber. It's a bustling place, with slaves unloading cargoes, and scribes busily recording every last *amphora* of olive oil.

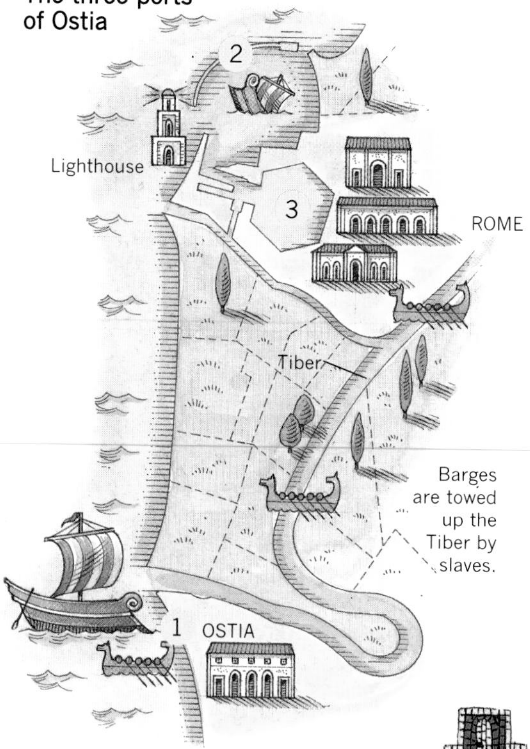

Government officials are on hand to direct operations and merchants, or their stewards, hover nearby, keeping an eagle eye on their investments.

THREE PORTS IN ONE

As it's 25 times cheaper to send goods by sea than land, the port sees huge business. With hundreds of ships coming and going, the original port 1 couldn't cope, so two more were built: one begun by Claudius in AD42, the most recent by Trajan in AD103. But Claudius' port 2 was open to the weather and in AD62, 200 ships sank, after taking shelter from a storm. Trajan's port 3 – shaped like a hexagon – can safely moor more than 300 ships at a time.

ART AT YOUR FEET

One of the most popular art forms in Rome is mosaics: pictures made from tiny tiles. Ostia has a fine example of mosaic art right under your feet. Look for it in the **Square of Corporations** near the playhouse. The Square houses the various businesses which operate from the port. Mosaics on the street outside their offices advertise their trades.

The three ports of Ostia

Lighthouse

2

3

ROME

Tiber

Barges are towed up the Tiber by slaves.

1   OSTIA

Mosaics of boats on the road tell you that a shipping company is nearby.

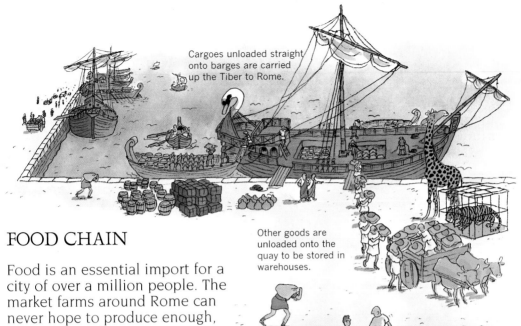

Cargoes unloaded straight onto barges are carried up the Tiber to Rome.

Other goods are unloaded onto the quay to be stored in warehouses.

FOOD CHAIN

Food is an essential import for a city of over a million people. The market farms around Rome can never hope to produce enough, so food, mainly grain, is brought in from other parts of the Empire. Grain from Africa, Egypt and Syria, weighing more than 40,000 elephants, passes through Ostia each year on its way to Rome.

> 66 *All that trade and ships may bring reaches Rome ...*
> *... So many cargoes arrive, that the city seems like a common warehouse of the world.* 99
>
> *Aelius Aristides*

IMPORTS

Grain forms just a tiny part of Rome's vast import trade, with huge quantities of goods arriving every day. Spain alone supplies a variety of food – olive oil, fruit, honey and salt fish – as well as wax, wool and cloth, silver, lead and red dye. Marble and purple dye come from Greece, papyrus (for books) from Egypt, spices and gems from India, silks from the Far East, glass from Syria, and amber from the Baltic.

BOAT-SPOTTING

The largest cargo ships can be up to 30m (100ft) long and 9m (30ft) wide, and are designed to hold immense cargoes. A ship might be carrying 6,000 *amphorae* full of wine, a weighty load of timber, or giraffes for the Games. Reliant on the wind to power their huge sails, ships can reach a top speed of only 7km an hour (just over 4 miles an hour). No wonder it can take up to three weeks to get from North Africa to Rome.

A WEEK IN THE COUNTRY

If the heat of the city gets to you, and you feel like a change, do as the Romans do and head to the country. You may meet someone who invites you to stay, or even offers to lend you their *villa* (country house) for a week or two.

After the city crowds and grime, you'll think you are in another world. Villas can be magnificent affairs: spacious houses, set in landscaped gardens, with pools, fountains and statues.

LIFE ON THE FARM

City people idealize country life and certainly, as the guest of a wealthy villa owner, you'll have a restful break. Such villas are actually lavish farmhouses, however. For the slaves who work on them, the harsh reality is long hours of back-breaking toil.

Most villas have an orchard to provide fresh fruit such as plums and figs.

Estates contain everything the family needs to be self-sufficient: living quarters, stabling, rooms to store crops – even a bakery and bath house.

Stabling for animals is at the back of the villa.

In front of the villa and within its walls, are formal gardens. The fields for crops are some distance from the house.

Inside, villas are richly decorated. This 'window' is part of a wall painting.

FARM PRODUCE

Cereals, grapes for wine, and olives for oil are the crops most often grown for sale by Roman farmers. They grow fruit and vegetables too, but these are for the dozens of people living and working on the estate. Fruit and vegetables for commercial use are produced by the numerous market gardeners on the outskirts of Rome. Ducks, chickens and geese are also raised, solely to supply the estate's needs.

COUNTRY FOOD

Country estates often have a pond to provide fresh fish for the dinner table, and the surrounding countryside offers a ready supply of game, including deer, boar and pheasant. Oxen are kept too, both for working in the wheat fields and for their leather hides.

WINE BUFFS

If grapes are the main crop at the estate where you're staying, you may get to see them harvested and processed – though watching wine-making may put you off the finished product. Once the grapes have been picked, they are poured into a stone vat and trampled on by barefooted slaves, to extract as much juice as possible. The last drops are then squeezed out with a press, before the liquid is stored in jars to ferment.

Slaves stuck with this sticky task hold onto poles to keep themselves from slipping.

The liquid either goes straight into jars or, when produced on a larger scale, is piped into another vat first.

TOP TIPS FOR TOURISTS
No. 19: Getting there

If you don't have a friend who will lend you their carriage for a week, you can rent a wagon at the city gates. You will need to allow several days for your journey, but there are various state-run guesthouses along the way, for overnight stops.

HEALTH SPAS

Many villas have bath houses attached, but for an extra lift, you could visit a mineral bath, offering smelly but revitalizing treatments.

BESIDE THE SEASIDE

If your villa is anywhere near the coast, it's worth extending your vacation to go to the seaside. The resorts of Capri and Naples are particularly popular, and their villas are often the last word in luxury. The beaches are clean, the sea inviting and, in Capri, there are regular boat trips for visitors around the bay.

> 66 *Why tire yourself in Rome, always bowing down to wealthy patrons*; *when you can be rich with the spoils of the woods and fields?* 99
> *Martial*

*Patrons are wealthy Romans who offer financial help and protection to poorer citizens, or those without families, in return for their political support.

RELIGION AND FESTIVALS

All life in Rome is closely connected with religion. There's a god or goddess (or minor spirit) for almost any activity you can think of. Religion itself is very much divided between public (or state) and private.

STATE RELIGION

State religion, run by paid priests and priestesses, is based around rituals performed at elaborate ceremonies. These are held in the sacred spaces in front of temples. People only enter if they have a special request. Inside, temples house treasure, gifts from worshippers and statues.

A statue of Jupiter

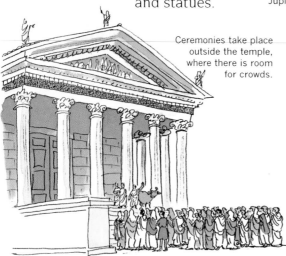

Ceremonies take place outside the temple, where there is room for crowds.

State worship focuses on *Roma*, goddess of Rome, other state deities (see right), and deified dead emperors. The state even tolerates foreign deities: the Romans are so anxious not to offend any gods in existence, they often take on those of their defeated enemies.

GODS & GODDESSES

Listed below are some of the most important state deities:-

Jupiter: King of the gods

Juno: Jupiter's wife, the goddess of women and marriage

Juno, often shown with a peacock

Minerva: Goddess of war and wisdom

Mars: God of war

Venus: Goddess of love and beauty

Mercury: God of trade and thieves, and Jupiter's messenger

Vesta: Goddess of the hearth

Mercury, with his winged sandals and voyager's clothes

EASTERN CULTS

As the empire grows, so has the popularity of cults from abroad, such as that of Isis, a goddess from Egypt. Christianity is increasingly popular, but is fiercely opposed by the state because Christians believe in only one god. Avoid all contact with Christians if you value your life.

PRIVATE RELIGION

Religion in the home is based around prayers. Each household has its own spirit, or *Lar*, to protect it and a shrine, the *Lararium*, where the family prays and offers small gifts of fruit and wine. Each family also has a *genius* (guardian spirit) and *manes* (ancestral spirits) to watch over them. There are even spirits of the pantry, called *penates*.

TELLING THE FUTURE

The Romans are great believers in supernatural forces, consulting all kinds of experts to tell them what the gods think of their plans. You could try it – but don't take it too seriously.

Haruspex: a priest who examines the innards of sacrificed animals to look for signs of disease. A damaged liver might show that the gods disapprove of a project.

A bronze plaque of an haruspex

Augurs: 16 prophets who look for ominous signs in nature, by studying things such as cloud shapes, flocks of birds or lightning.

Sibyl: a prophetess who wrote books during the early Republic, with advice on interpreting the will of the gods.

Astrologers: tell a person's fortune, by studying the position of the stars at the time of his birth.

CALENDAR OF FESTIVALS

There are over 200 festivals, only a few of which can be listed, so your trip is bound to coincide with one.

FEB 15 **Lupercalia**
At a cave on the Palatine, two teams put on goatskins and race around the hill.

MAR 15 **Anna Perenna, goddess of the year**
Take a picnic to the Tiber – with plenty to drink. Romans believe the more they drink on this day, the longer they'll live.

APR 21 **Parilia**
Traditionally, the day of Rome's birth. Each area of the city organizes a celebration, including bonfires and large outdoor feasts.

APR 28 **Ludi Florales**
A carnival for Flora, goddess of flowers (one to avoid if you get hayfever). Everyone dances in floral garlands.

JUN 9 **Vestalia**
A festival for Vesta. Note: the bakeries will be shut. The Vestal Virgins bake a special bread for the day, so bakers take the day off.

AUG 12 **Feast of Mercury**
A massive – and free – public feast. It's funded from the 10% businessmen pay to Mercury's shrine from their profits each year.

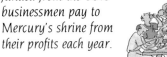

SEP 5-19 **Ludi Romani**
A festival of games, races and plays. If you're invited to the banquet at the Senate, don't be surprised if some guests are rather quiet. Statues of gods are dressed up and put on couches to join in.

49

FASHION

STYLE

Most clothes for men and women are based around simple shapes and usually made from a large, rectangular piece of cloth. This is folded to be worn and held in place with a brooch called a *fibula*, or tied with a belt and buckle. As all sewing is done by hand, the Romans do as little as possible.

A Roman soldier's buckle

FABRIC

Clothes are generally made of wool or linen. Fine linen and silks are imported from Egypt and Greece, but they're extremely expensive and worn only by the seriously wealthy. Men tend to wear clothes in their natural state of cream, or bleached white, but women wear a variety of shades. Vegetable and mineral dyes are used to brighten cloth. The richer you are, the brighter and more varied your clothes.

HIS . . .

Underneath it all, men wear a loincloth. This is the only underwear they bother with and it's generally kept on at night. Over the top, they wear a simple tunic. The tunic is designed to hang slightly longer at the back than the front, which ends at the knee. Outside, they also wear cloaks.

Togas are only worn by Roman citizens and their sons. They're very heavy, not to mention tricky to wear. Try carrying on a conversation while shifting yards of cloth over a shoulder.

Togas are always white. To brighten things up for a party, men can wear cloaks in funkier shades; they wear dark, if not black, cloaks for solemn occasions such as funerals.

Older men wear longer tunics. The purple stripe shows that the wearer is a Senator.

Putting on a toga

This is a complicated and time-consuming business. For those occasions where you have to wear one, here's the simple way to put it on:

1. Drape over the left shoulder.

2. Bring the other end in front of you.

3. Throw it over your left shoulder.

4. Tuck a section into your belt.

... AND HERS

Women also wear simple underwear with a plain tunic on top. Over that, they wear a long dress called a *stola*. These are plain too, although wealthier women wear *stolas* of silk in dazzling shades including red, yellow, purple and blue. Dressier *stolas*, with elaborate embroidery, are worn on special occasions.

A *stola*

On top of the *stola*, many women wear a *palla*, a long, rectangular scarf. When out of the house, most women cover themselves up, either with a veil or by wearing the *palla* draped over their heads.

The *palla* is worn like a large shawl, wrapped around the body and thrown over one shoulder.

COSMETICS

Pale skin is very much in vogue, so arms and faces are whitened with powdered chalk. Ash is used to darken eyelids and eyebrows; lips and cheeks are reddened with plant dye or the sediment from red wine.

CHILDREN

Clothes for children pretty much match those for adults. The very young run around in short tunics. But, from an early age, the sons of citizens wear a mini toga, called a *toga praetexta*, and girls a *stola*.

HAIR

For Roman men, the term "fashion victim" has as much – and painful – relevance as for women. Though hairstyles are simple (most men sport a close crop), they face the daily torture of a visit to the barber for a shave.

Blunt iron razors, and only water on the face beforehand, mean cuts are an unavoidable hazard. If you decide to risk a visit, you might like to bear in mind this cure to stop bleeding: spiders' webs soaked in oil and vinegar.

Poorer women pull their hair back into plain buns, but the rich suffer long hours having their hair dressed – piled high upon their heads and teased into ringlets or braids. If hair isn't naturally curly, heated tongs are used.

Blonde and red hair are currently the most fashionable. Rather than resort to dye, some women simply have a wig made from the blonde or red hair of a slave.

Dozens of hair pins, which can be made of ivory, silver, or bone like this one, hold intricate hairstyles in place.

EDUCATION

SCHOOLING

In education, as in everything else, there is a sharp divide between rich and poor. Most families can't afford to educate their offspring, sending them out to work instead. Only the children of wealthy parents are educated. The richest have a private tutor. For the rest – boys and girls – the first school, or *ludus*, begins at the age of six and lasts until they're 11.

THE *LUDUS*

The *ludus* usually consists of one room, on the ground floor of a *domus* or behind a shop. The school day begins at dawn and continues until noon without a break, quite a strain for the youngest pupils. Classes are small with, on average, 12 pupils per class. Most schools have one class and one teacher, often a Greek ex-slave. Schools vary but each has set fees – parents pick the one they can afford.

DISCIPLINE

Teachers are strict disciplinarians and ardent supporters of corporal punishment, with beatings a regular occurrence.

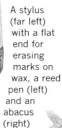

A family slave called a *pedagogus* takes children to and from school, and keeps an eye on them while they're there.

EQUIPMENT

Young pupils scratch their first letters on pieces of broken pottery, or wax tablets, using a metal pen called a *stylus*. Older pupils write on sheets of papyrus (see right), using reed pens, and ink made from a mixture of gum and soot. Arithmetic is equally low-tech. It's taught using fingers and an abacus.

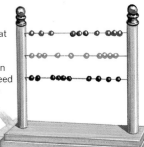

A stylus (far left) with a flat end for erasing marks on wax, a reed pen (left) and an abacus (right)

LESSONS

Lessons cover the basics: reading, writing and simple arithmetic. One of the most common teaching tools is reciting – the alphabet for the youngest children; the works of famous Greek and Roman authors for older pupils.

THE *GRAMMATICUS*

Exclusively for boys, and exclusive in every other sense, the *grammaticus* covers the secondary stage of education. It takes boys only, from the richest parents, from the age of 11 until at least 13 or 14. Most girls marry at 12, so they leave the *ludus* to learn how to run a household.

THE CURRICULUM

At first sight, the curriculum at the *grammaticus* seems wide-ranging, covering history and geography, mythology, astronomy, music and mathematics. But most of the day is taken up with studying Greek *odes* (long story-telling poems), because Greek culture has such a major influence on Roman life. Many lessons consist simply of reading aloud or reciting passages which have already been learned by heart. (Dull for pupils but worse for visitors, if you were planning to visit a school.)

A carving of a boy reciting

PUBLIC SPEAKING

Public speaking is a vital part of schooling for anyone who wants to go into law or politics. From about 13, some boys are sent to a *rhetor* to learn the art of speaking in public.

Boys are taught how to write and present speeches, using various exercises. One involves saying the same thing in a dozen different ways. The *rhetor* also dreams up bizarre scenarios for his pupils to debate. Training can last for years, with the luckiest being sent to Athens or Rhodes to finish their education.

CITIZEN TRAINING

The main role of the secondary stage of education, however, is to train upper class boys to take their place as Roman citizens, and prepare them for the task of ruling Rome and the Empire.

MAKING 'PAPER'

Papyrus, made from an Egyptian reed, is the Roman form of paper. Quality varies, the best coming from the middle of the papyrus pith. It goes through four stages before you can write on it:

1   With the outer rind of the reed removed, the core is cut into strips and soaked in water.

2   Two layers of strips are pressed together at right angles. Starch in the core acts like glue.

3   The sheet is beaten with a mallet and left to dry, before being polished with a stone.

4   Lots of sheets are joined together to form a scroll. In a well-made scroll, the joins are invisible.

Pupils unrolling a scroll: since scrolls are around 10m (30ft) long, they're often fitted with wooden or ivory rollers to make them easier to handle.

THE ARMY

EMPIRE BUILDERS

It's thanks to Rome's army that the Empire has reached the size and stature it has, while constant warfare with countries on all its borders has made the army an efficient and destructive fighting force.

FIGHTING FARMERS

Initially, all Roman property-owners (usually farmers) had to serve in the army. Wars were brief and near Rome, so it was almost a vacation – though a violent one to which you took your own weapons. But, soon, a more dedicated body of men was required. By 100BC, men no longer needed property to join. Soldiers were paid, and given a uniform, weapons and training.

A HARD LIFE

Life in the army is tough. Minor infringements result in flogging. Trouble-makers have their rations reduced, but in a mutinous legion, every tenth man is executed (the origin of the term "to decimate").

Route marches of 30km (18 miles) take place three times a month. Troops have to march at up to 8km (5 miles) an hour, carrying heavy packs, to prepare them for long marches on campaigns.

A cooking pot is just one of the many items in a soldier's pack.

AN ARMY CAMP

At the end of a long day's march, soldiers have to build the overnight camp, so camps go up quickly and always in the same form:

All camps are square. Inside, the tents are pitched in rows.

The General's headquarters is always in the middle of the camp.

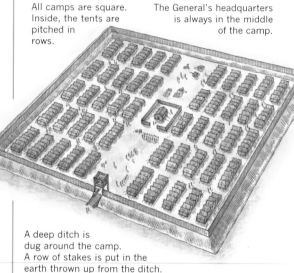

A deep ditch is dug around the camp. A row of stakes is put in the earth thrown up from the ditch.

WEAPONS

Standard weapons issue includes: a short stabbing sword, 60cm (2ft) long, hung from the right side of the belt; a dagger, hung from the left; and two *pila* (javelins), one heavy, one light. These have wooden shafts with a middle section of soft iron, deliberately designed to bend as the spear hits its target. This is to prevent the enemy from throwing them back.

A dagger in a decorated scabbard: this would belong to a general or someone of a fairly high rank.

UNIFORM

Every soldier receives a uniform, though the cost is deducted from his pay. The basic get-up is the same for all: a wool or linen tunic, with wool breeches and a cloak in colder climates. Tunics are topped with a belted shirt of fine chain mail, or a more protective leather tunic with metal strips. Everyone wears a metal helmet and carries a curved wooden and leather shield. Some soldiers also wear metal leg protectors.

Soldiers generally wear sandals. These are replaced with sturdy boots for marches.

ARMY DIVISIONS

Much of the army's success relies on its structured nature. 28 groups called **legions**, each with around 5,000 men, are divided into smaller groups, down to a group of eight men called a *contubernium*.

A *contubernium*: 8 men who share a tent and eat together.

10 *contubernia* make up 1 **century** of 80 men.

Centuries group together to form **cohorts**. Each legion is made up of 10 cohorts. The **First Cohort** has 10 centuries (800 men). The other nine have 6 centuries (480 men).

LEGIONS

Legions don't just contain soldiers, but doctors, clerks, priests, engineers and surveyors. They also have auxiliaries, non-citizens from the provinces, who are grouped in cohorts of 500 to 1,000 men. These earn less than legionaries and have less training. They often provide the cavalry, acting as scouts and carrying messages.

A senior officer called a **legate** commands each legion. Below him are six officers called **tribunes**. Each century is led by a **centurion**, who is assisted by an **optio**.

PERSONALITIES

Aquilifer: carries the legion's standard into battle, wearing a lion skin over his uniform.

Signifer: carries the century's standard; organizes the burial club for soldiers' funerals.

Praefectus castrorum: in charge of building camps; third in command after the *legate* and senior *tribune*.

Tesserarius: the army spy. Each century has a daily password, which the *tesserarius* gives the soldiers each morning.

A standard: if a legion's standard is captured, the legion is disgraced and disbanded, so a cunning enemy makes straight for the *Aquilifer*.

USEFUL INFORMATION

CURRENCY

During the Republic, various Roman mints each produced their own coins. Thanks to Augustus, the monetary system is standardized now and all coins have a fixed value. The most recent will show Trajan's or Hadrian's head, but coins issued under earlier emperors are still acceptable.

Aureus: gold - weighs 8g (¼ oz); the largest denomination

Denarius: silver - 25 *denarii* in an *aureus*

Sestertius: bronze - 4 *sestertii* in a *denarius*

Dupondius: bronze - 2 *dupondii* in a *sestertius*

As: copper - 4 *as* in a *sestertius*

Semi: bronze - 2 *semis* in an *as*

Quadrans: copper - 4 *quadrans* in an *as*

NUMBERS

Roman numerals are made up of a combination of the letters I, V, X, L, C, D and M. They follow a logical pattern, based on addition and subtraction. 4, for example, is written IV, meaning 1 less than 5 (V); 7 is VII, or 5 (V) plus 2 (II). But since all numbers are based around just a few letters, you are soon dealing with very long numbers. For example, it takes seven letters to write 78:

50 + 20 + 5 + 3 = 78

Numbers in Latin*:

1 **I**	11 **XI**		
2 **II**	12 **XII**	50	**L**
3 **III**	13 **XIII**		
4 **IV**	14 **XIV**	100	**C**
5 **V**	15 **XV**		
6 **VI**	16 **XVI**	200	**CC**
7 **VII**	17 **XVII**	500	**D**
8 **VIII**	18 **XVIII**		
9 **IX**	19 **XIX**	1000	**M**
10 **X**	20 **XX**		

1	*unus*	8	*octo*
2	*duo*	9	*novem*
3	*tres*	10	*decem*
4	*quattuor*	11	*undecem*
5	*quinque*	12	*duodecem*
6	*sex*	50	*quinquaginta*
7	*septem*	100	*centum*

*See page 59 for tips on how to pronounce Latin

TIME

Telling the time in Ancient Rome is a vague business. Romans rely on sundials and water clocks to tell the time, but neither are very accurate. Days last as long as the daylight and are divided into twelve hours.

Sundial

Midday falls exactly in the middle – the point at which the sixth hour gives way to the seventh. Hours are approximate, not subdivided into minutes, and longer in the summer, when the light lasts longer.

LAUNDRY

If you have a toga, it will need specialist dry-cleaning. You can send your toga and other dirty washing to a fuller. Fullers generally treat cloth before it's made into clothes, but they also offer a cleaning service.

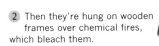

1 First, togas are trodden in a mixture of sodium-carbonate and a type of clay known as "fuller's earth".

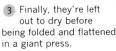

2 Then they're hung on wooden frames over chemical fires, which bleach them.

3 Finally, they're left out to dry before being folded and flattened in a giant press.

EMERGENCIES

Since 6AD, a combined police and fire-fighting force called the *Cohortes Vigilum* has been in operation. They'll be on hand if your apartment catches fire, but don't expect them to do two jobs at once if your valuables are stolen.

Firemen use leather buckets and hoses.

MAIL

There's no postal service for ordinary citizens, but government mail is sent by courier. You could try charm or a bribe to have urgent letters included with the official mail. But it's really not worth it if you're only sending postcards home – they'll arrive months after you, if they arrive at all.

NEWSPAPERS

If you're fluent in Latin, a daily paper called the Acta Diurna – actually a single handwritten sheet – is handed out in the Forum with the latest news.

PHRASEBOOK & DEFINITIONS

HANDY WORDS AND PHRASES

Hello	*salve or salvete**
Goodbye	*vale or valete**

Add **domine** (sir) for a man and **domina** (madam) for a woman.

How are you?	*ut vales?*
I'm well	*bene valeo*
Very well	*optime*
Quite well	*satis bene*
Not very well	*non ita bene*
Terrible	*pessime*

Yes	*ita est*
Thank you	*gratias ago*
Tell me	*dic mihi*
I don't know	*non scio*
I'm sorry	*doleo*

I would like	*velim*
I don't like	*displicet mihi*
I don't want	*nolo*
I prefer	*praefero*

When is...?	*quando ... est?*
What are...?	*quod ... sunt?*
What is this?	*quid hoc est?*
Why?	*cur?*
Who?	*quis?*
How?	*ut?*
How many?	*quot?*
Here is...	*ecce ...*
There are...	*ibi ... sunt*

Not	*non*
Not at all	*minime*
But	*sed*
Also	*etiam*
And	*et* or *que* on the end of a word

FIND YOUR WAY AROUND

Excuse me	*da mihi veniam*
Where is...?	*ubi ... est?*
How do I get to?	*qua via venio ad?*
Straight ahead	*in directum*
Nearby	*in propinquo*
On the left	*a laeva parte*
On the right	*a dextra parte*
Is it far?	*estne longinquum?*

FOOD AND SHOPPING

Food	*cibaria*
Bakery	*pistrina*
Butcher's shop	*laniena*
Milk	*lac*
Eggs	*ova*
Fruit	*pomum*
Vegetables	*holera*
Meat	*caro*
Fish	*piscis*
Bread	*panis*
Lettuce	*lactuca*
Sausage	*botulus*
Cheese	*caseus*
Roll or bun	*panicellus*
Water	*aqua*

I eat	*edo*
I'm hungry	*esurio*

What do you want?	*quid requiris?*
I want...	*requiro...*
What else?	*quid alium?*
Nothing now	*nihil iam*
How much does ... cost?	*quanti constat...?*
How much do ... cost?	*quanti constant...?*

*Use *salvete* and *valete* when you are talking to more than one person.

DAYS OF THE WEEK

Monday	*dies Lunae*
Tuesday	*dies Martis*
Wednesday	*dies Mercurii*
Thursday	*dies Iovis*
Friday	*dies Veneris*
Saturday	*dies Saturni*
Sunday	*dies Solis*

MONTHS OF THE YEAR

January	*Januarius*
February	*Februarius*
March	*Martius*
April	*Aprilis*
May	*Maius*
June	*Junius*
July	*Julius*
August	*Augustus*
September	*September**
October	*October**
November	*November**
December	*December**

*Until Julius Caesar changed the calendar, March began the year. This made September, October, November and December, the seventh (*septem*), eighth (*octo*), ninth (*novem*) and tenth (*decem*) months.

PRONUNCIATION TIPS

Pronunciation is easy – for nearly every letter, say it as it is written. There are just three exceptions:
'c' is pronounced like a 'k'
'v' is pronounced like a 'w'
'i' before a vowel is pronounced like a 'y'
Examples:
for *panicellus* (bread) say *pani-kellus*
for *novem* (nine) say *no-wem*
for *iam* (now) say *yam*

USEFUL DEFINITIONS

aqueduct: a channel for carrying water, often carried on a bridge, also called an aqueduct.

basilica: a large public building, in or near the **forum**, housing law courts, offices and shops.

citizen: originally, a man born in Rome to Roman parents, who could vote and serve in the army. (By late Republican times, citizenship was being offered to those considered worthy of it and, by Hadrian's time, it was extended to many people across the Empire.)

consul: the most senior government official. Two consuls are elected annually to run the affairs of the **Senate** and command the armies.

domus: a private house.

emperor: supreme ruler of all Roman territories. Augustus became the first emperor in 27BC.

Empire: **(1)** the extent of Roman territories; **(2)** the period from 27BC to 476AD when Rome was ruled by emperors.

Etruscans: people who lived in north-west Italy and flourished before the Romans came to power. In its early days, Rome was ruled by Etruscan kings.

forum: an open space in the middle of a Roman town, used for markets, law courts and politics.

hypocaust: central heating – hot air flows through gaps between walls and under floors.

Imperial Rome: the period when Rome was ruled by emperors.

insula: an apartment block – each apartment within the block is called a *cenaculum*.

republic: a state or country without a king, queen or emperor, whose leaders have been elected into power by the people. Rome was a republic from the 6th century BC until 27BC.

Senate: the group of nobles that governs Rome. By 82BC, there were 600 senators. The Senate's powers are gradually being reduced, as emperors take more power for themselves.

slave: a person with no rights, owned by another. Most slaves are prisoners-of-war.

viaduct: a bridge which carries a road across a river or a valley.

villa: a large house or estate in the country.

WHO'S WHO IN ANCIENT ROME

STRUCTURE OF SOCIETY

Roman society consists of two groups: citizens, called *cives*, and non-citizens. Eligibility for citizenship has varied over the years; it's now far less strict (see page 59). Citizens enjoy many rights and privileges not open to non-citizens. These include voting in elections and the outdated – and more dubious – right to serve in the army.

CITIZENS

Within the rank of citizen there are three divisions:

Patricians: the richest citizens, who make up the ruling class.

Equites: descended from the first Roman cavalry officers, modern *equites* are businessmen and bankers.

Plebeians (commoners): the poorest citizens, probably descended from peasant farmers and craftsmen.

NON-CITIZENS

Non-citizens are divided into:

Provincials: people from Roman territories who don't yet have citizenship. Denied the full rights of citizens, they also have to pay taxes to the Roman government, from which citizens are exempt.

Foreigners: all those from outside the Empire.

Slaves: owned by other people and bought and sold like property.

POETS AND POLITICIANS

Below are just some of the many notable people in Roman history. (See the timeline on pages 62-63 for a list of the main Emperors.) Names in **bold** have their own entry in the list. Terms with an asterisk (*) are defined on page 59.

Augustus (31BC-AD14; Emperor* 27BC-AD14): the name taken by **Octavian**, great-nephew of **Julius Caesar**, when he became the first Roman Emperor in 27BC. Augustus took control after years of civil war, bringing peace and prosperity to Rome.

Caesar, Julius (c.100-44BC): a politician, soldier and writer, who extended Roman territory as far as Britain. In 46BC, he defeated his political opponents and was declared dictator. But the Senate* feared he would make himself king and, on March 15 44BC, had him murdered.

Cato (234-149BC): a politician and writer whose book *De agri cultura* is the oldest existing work of Latin prose.

Catullus (c.84-c.54BC): a poet who wrote love poems and vivid descriptions of Roman life. Catullus was the first to adopt the forms of Greek poetry.

Cicero (106-43BC): a politician, lawyer and writer who was renowned as the best public speaker of his day.

Domitian (AD51-96; Emperor AD81-96): a strong and arrogant ruler who strengthened Rome's frontiers and restored many public buildings. Anyone who opposed him was murdered. He was eventually assassinated.

Hadrian (AD76-138; Emperor AD117-138): a scholar and soldier who spent much time with armies in the provinces, building barriers (including Hadrian's Wall in Britain) against invaders. He also built a library in Greece and a palace, Hadrian's Villa, near Rome.

Horace (65-8BC): a poet, famous for his *Odes*, short poems on topics such as food, wine and the countryside.

Juvenal (c.AD60-c.130): a poet whose *Satires* criticized the poverty, immorality and injustices of Roman life.

Livy (59BC-AD17): a historian who wrote *Ab urbe condita*, a vast history of Rome and its people.

Mark Antony (82-30BC): a soldier and politician who was a consul* with **Caesar** in 44BC. After a brief alliance with **Octavian**, war broke out between them. Mark Antony committed suicide after his defeat by Octavian in 30BC.

Martial (c.AD40-104): a poet who wrote *Epigrams*, short poems about Rome's more lively characters and everyday life.

Nero (AD37-68; Emperor AD54-68): an emperor so obsessed with power, he had all those who opposed him killed, including his mother, Agrippina. He is said to have caused a fire in AD64 which destroyed much of Rome. Finally, he was forced to commit suicide.

Nerva (c.AD30-98; Emperor AD96-98): an emperor who treated the Senate with respect, and introduced the system whereby emperors chose and trained their replacements.

Octavian: see **Augustus**

Ovid (43BC-AD18): a poet whose most famous work is *Metamorphoses*, fifteen books of poems on myths and legends.

Pliny (c.AD61-c.113): a writer and lawyer who published the letters he exchanged with **Trajan** and **Tacitus**, among others.

Plutarch (AD46-126): author of *Plutarch's Lives*, pairs of biographies comparing the lives of Greek and Roman soldiers and statesmen.

Seneca (c.5BC-AD65): a writer, lawyer and philosopher, he was also **Nero**'s tutor and was forced to commit suicide when they fell out.

Suetonius (c.AD69-140): a historian and government official who wrote *Lives of the Twelve Caesars*, on the lives and careers of twelve rulers from **Caesar** to **Domitian**.

Tacitus (c.AD55-c.116): a historian and consul* who wrote the *Annals* and the *Histories* about the lives of emperors.

Terence (c.195-159BC): a playwright who adapted Greek comedies. Originally a slave, he was freed by his master.

Trajan (c.AD53-117; Emperor AD98-117): a superb soldier and general, under whom the Empire* grew to its largest extent. Among his many public buildings were baths, basilicas* and a forum*

Vespasian (AD9-79; Emperor AD70-79): the emperor who restored order after **Nero**, and began extensive public building works, including the Colosseum.

Virgil (70-19BC): a poet who spent the last ten years of his life writing his most celebrated poem *The Aeneid*, the story of the history of Rome in twelve books.

TIMELINE OF ANCIENT ROME

Names in **bold** are referred to on pages 60-61.

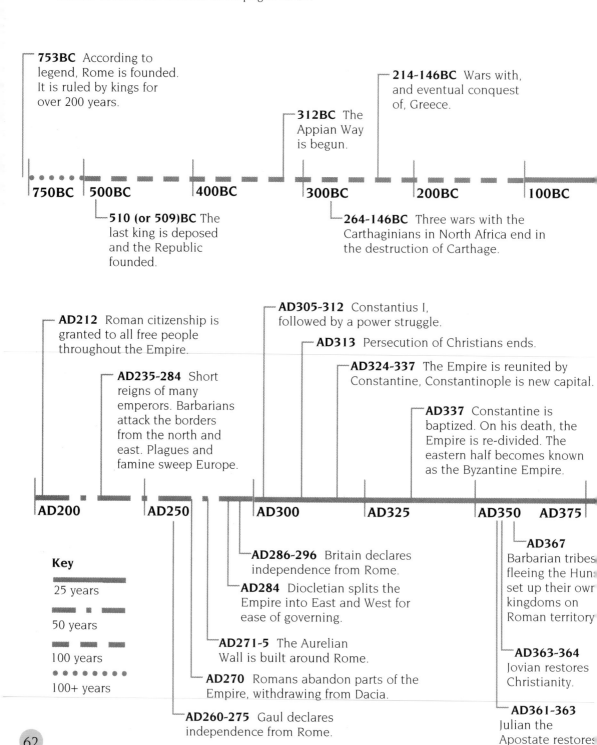

753BC According to legend, Rome is founded. It is ruled by kings for over 200 years.

214-146BC Wars with, and eventual conquest of, Greece.

312BC The Appian Way is begun.

750BC   **500BC**   **400BC**   **300BC**   **200BC**   **100BC**

510 (or 509)BC The last king is deposed and the Republic founded.

264-146BC Three wars with the Carthaginians in North Africa end in the destruction of Carthage.

AD212 Roman citizenship is granted to all free people throughout the Empire.

AD305-312 Constantius I, followed by a power struggle.

AD313 Persecution of Christians ends.

AD235-284 Short reigns of many emperors. Barbarians attack the borders from the north and east. Plagues and famine sweep Europe.

AD324-337 The Empire is reunited by Constantine, Constantinople is new capital.

AD337 Constantine is baptized. On his death, the Empire is re-divided. The eastern half becomes known as the Byzantine Empire.

AD200   **AD250**   **AD300**   **AD325**   **AD350**   **AD375**

AD367 Barbarian tribes fleeing the Huns set up their own kingdoms on Roman territory.

Key

25 years

50 years

100 years

100+ years

AD286-296 Britain declares independence from Rome.

AD284 Diocletian splits the Empire into East and West for ease of governing.

AD271-5 The Aurelian Wall is built around Rome.

AD270 Romans abandon parts of the Empire, withdrawing from Dacia.

AD363-364 Jovian restores Christianity.

AD260-275 Gaul declares independence from Rome.

AD361-363 Julian the Apostate restores the Roman gods.

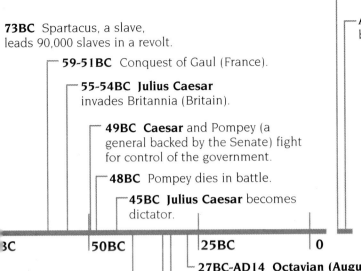

AD43 Conquest of Britain begins.

AD64 Rome burns down. **Nero** blames the Christians.

73BC Spartacus, a slave, leads 90,000 slaves in a revolt.

AD68-9 On **Nero**'s death, power struggles lead to civil war.

59-51BC Conquest of Gaul (France).

55-54BC Julius Caesar invades Britannia (Britain).

AD69 Vespasian's rule: a period of prosperity and military success for Rome.

49BC Caesar and Pompey (a general backed by the Senate) fight for control of the government.

AD122 Hadrian's wall is begun.

48BC Pompey dies in battle.

45BC Julius Caesar becomes dictator.

3C | 50BC | 25BC | 0 | AD100 AD200

27BC-AD14 Octavian (Augustus) is declared the first emperor. The Roman Empire begins.

AD117 The Empire is at its largest, with conquests of Dacia and Parthia.

31BC Octavian defeats **Mark Antony** and Cleopatra.

c. 33BC Octavian and **Mark Antony** fight for control.

AD79 The Colosseum opens. Vesuvius erupts.

44BC Julius Caesar is assassinated. Civil wars follow.

AD392-395 Theodosius reunites the Empire.

AD455 Vandals invade Italy from Africa and destroy Rome.

AD394 Christianity is the state religion

AD400 | AD450 | AD500 | AD1453

Constantinople is overrun by the Turks.

AD410 Rome is sacked by Goths; Britain and Gaul are abandoned.

AD476 Romulus Augustus (West), is deposed by Odoacer, a barbarian captain. The Eastern Empire is ruled from Constantinople under the Byzantine emperors.

AD402 Goths invade Italy. The Imperial court moves from Rome to Ravenna.

ROMAN EMPERORS

27BC-AD14	Augustus
AD14-37	Tiberius
AD37-41	Caligula
AD41-54	Claudius
AD54-68	Nero
AD69	Galba; Otho; Vitellius
AD69-79	Vespasian
AD79-81	Titus
AD81-96	Domitian
AD96-98	Nerva
AD98-117	Trajan
AD117-138	Hadrian
AD138-161	Antoninus Pius
AD161-180	Marcus Aurelius
AD180-192	Commodus
AD193-211	Septimus Severus
AD211-217	Caracalla
AD217-218	Macrinus
AD218-222	Elagabalus
AD222-235	Severus Alexander
AD284-305	Diocletian (East)
AD286-305	Maximinian (West)
AD312-337	Constantine
AD337-361	Constantine's sons
AD361-364	Julian the Apostate; Jovian
AD364-379	Valentinian I; Valens; Gratian; Valentinian II
AD379-392	Theodosius (East)
AD395-423	Honorius

INDEX

(*Emperors are in* **bold**)
actor, 28-9, 34
Aesculapius, 18, 43
amphora, 37, 44
Annona, 43
Appian Way, see
  Via Appia
aqueduct, 7, 9,
  14-15, 30, 33
architecture, 30-1
  arches, 20, 24,
  30, 33
  columns, 23, 30
  domes, 12, 14,
  30-1
  vaults, 30
army, 54-5
Augustus, 22-3,
  33, 56, 60, 63

baker, 9, 37, 46,
  49, 58
banquet, 10-11
barges, 42, 44-5
basilica, 20-1, 22-3,
  59
baths, 7, 12-13,
  14-15, 47
books, 38-9
bread, 8-9, 11, 49

Caesar, Julius, 16,
  20-1, 22-3, 33,
  60, 63
catacombs, 35
chariot racing, 26-7
Circus Maximus, 26
citizen, 4, 26, 29,
  50, 53, 59, 60
Cloaca Maxima, 7,
  20
clothes, 5, 12,
  50-1, 57
Colosseum, 24-5, 62
cosmetics, 15, 39,
  51

currency, 56

days of the week,
  59
dentists, 19
doctors, 18-19
domus (town
  house), 6
drink, 5, 9, 11, 26

education, 52-3
emergencies, 57
emperor, 4, 20-1,
  27, 32, 48, 59,
  60-1, 62-3
Empire, 4, 45, 53,
  54, 59, 62-3

farming, 40, 46, 54
festivals, 49
food, 7, 8-9, 10-11,
  26, 37, 40-1
fora (forums), 20-1,
  22-3, 34, 36, 38-9,
  40-1, 43, 59
funerals, 34-5

games, 15, 24-5
gladiators, 25
glass, 38, 45
god(dess), 18,
  20-1, 31, 48-9
Greeks, 18, 30-1,
  38, 41, 45, 60-1,
  62

Hadrian, 4, 31,
  61, 63
hair, 15, 51
hypocaust, 15, 59

Imperial Fora, 20,
  22-3, 40
imports, 40, 45, 50
insula (apartment),
  6-7, 8, 41, 57

jewels, 39
Jupiter, 21, 48

laundry, 57
legion, 32, 54-5
litter (transport),
  16
markets, 5, 6, 12,
  22, 40-1, 43
medicine, 9, 18-19,
  43
military
  processions, 32-3
mime, 29
months, 59
mosaic, 44

newspapers, 57
numbers, 56

olive oil, 8, 12,
  36-7, 40, 42,
  44-5, 46
opening hours, 37
opticians, 18
Ostia, 42, 44-5

Pantheon, 31
papyrus, 53
plays, 28-9, 61
ports, 42, 44
post, 57
priest(ess), 27,
  48-9

religion, 18, 48-9
renting, 6
roads, 16-17, 32,
  35
Roman Forum,
  20-1, 22, 33, 38-9

Sacred Way, see
  Via Sacra
scales, 41

seaside, 47
Senate, 20-1, 49,
  59
sewers, 7, 20
ships, 42, 44-5
shoes, 37
shops, 6, 20, 22,
  36-7, 38-9, 40
slaves, 10, 11, 12,
  15, 16, 24, 32, 39,
  41, 43, 44, 46, 51,
  52
snack bars, 8
soldiers, 19, 32-3,
  54-5
standard, 32, 55
strigil, 12-13
surgery, 19

temples, 20-1,
  22-3, 31, 33, 48
time, 57
togas, 5, 26, 50
tombs, 34-5
transport, 16, 35,
  47
Trajan, 4, 22-3,
  33, 61, 63
  baths, 14
  column, 23
  forum, 22-3
  market, 40

uniform, 32, 55

Via Appia, 33, 35
Via Sacra, 32-3
villa, 46-7, 59

warehouses, 42-3
water, 5, 6-7, 9, 11,
  15, 16, 30, 33, 51,
  53, 57, 58
wine, 9, 11, 18, 26,
  39, 42, 46-7, 49,
  51